What reviewers say about Jo Peddicord and her first book, *Look Like A Winner After 50*:

"[Peddicord] believes in the lift looking good provides women, and she knows how to encourage women to take charge of their bodies. For Jo, looking good is one of the ways to create a healthy, confident spirit; it's not a superficial achievement...."
—Senior Messenger, Vancouver, WA

"Jo Peddicord is out to change opinions, and she is doing it by example as well as by words. New doors will be opened and new dreams realized if women strengthen the belief that they are useful and attractive at any age, she says. And she knows from personal experience."
— Mature Outlook Magazine

"[Peddicord] advises not to put any limitations on one's self just because of a number. Find out what looks good and what fits your lifestyle and go for it."
— The Fresno Bee

"Colorado writer, Jo Peddicord, who penned *Look Like A Winner After 50*, applauds older women who are changing their attitudes about aging. 'We are going from grow old gracefully to grow young period,' she says. 'This is not about vanity, ego or being glamorous when glamour isn't appropriate. It's about eating healthy, staying fit and updating our appearance.'"
— The Atlanta Journal / The Atlanta Constitution

"*Look Like A Winner After 50*" offers baby boomers to grandmothers proven and practical solutions to their special cosmetic and clothing needs, plus beauty-creating secrets...."
— Wisconsin Bookwatch

"[*Look Like A Winner*] is more than a primer for lipstick and blush. She hopes to send the message that great looks don't stop when you cross the half-century mark."
— Chicago Sun-Times

"The final chapter recommends that women who are discouraged or bored with the way they look should start by tossing out the 'old stuff' ⸱ ⸱ ⸱ ⸱ ⸱ ⸱ ⸱ ⸱ng about the new you....If w ⸱ ⸱ ⸱ Peddicord says."
—Th

azine

Feel Nifty After 50!

Top Tips to Help Women Grow Young!

by

Jo Peddicord

Golden Aspen Publishing

Published by:
Golden Aspen Publishing
Post Office Box 370333
Denver, CO 80237-0333, U.S.A.
(303) 694-6555
Fax: (303) 694-0737, Email: GAPub@aol.com

Edited by Lucy Beckstead
Cover design by George Foster
Cartoons by Andrew Toos

Publisher's Cataloging in Publication
(Provided by Quality books, Inc.)

Peddicord, Jo.
    "Feel nifty after 50! / top tips to help women grow young! /
Jo Peddicord. -- 1st ed.
        p. cm.
    Includes bibliographical references and index.
    LCCN: 98-93704
    ISBN 0-9654434-1-8

    1. Middle-aged women--Health and hygiene. 2. Aged
women--Health and hygiene. 3. Beauty, Personal. 4. Middle-aged
women--Conduct of life. 5. Aged women--Conduct of life.
I. Title.

RA778.P316 1999   646.7'042
                         QB198-1472

10 9 8 7 6 5 4 3 2 1
FIRST EDITION

Dedication

This book is dedicated to all women everywhere
who realize life is what we make it. Despite heartbreaking
experiences and trauma, they eternally make roses
grow out of the ashes and reach for the stars.
But, they are firmly grounded with the desire to
live, and help others to live, graciously.

Contents

Introduction to the Present and Future of Longevity

As the 20th century yields to the 21st, the concept of "growing young" instead of growing old is coming into full bloom. The seeds of this revolution sprouted in the mid 1980s with the publication of numerous books and articles on nutrition and fitness as useful solutions to healthy longevity. New times require new solutions.

Getting older is inevitable, but it is outdated to think of the second half of our lives as declining. Remember how many times George Burns, a great comedian of the 20th century, sang, said and wrote, "We can't help getting older, but we don't have to get old." At this time of life we can use our accumulated experience, knowledge and education to build adventurous, service- oriented and interesting lives. These are the years to extend our minds and tune up our physiques and appearance. Thousands of men and women, in this century and past, have made amazing accomplishments in their later years.

Stereotypes of the past no longer fit the over-50 crowd of today. Many of us feel 15 to 20 years younger than our age. Many are doing the same things they were doing in younger years with exciting plans for the future. Many look better now than they ever did. After working hard at growing up, they are now enjoying the benefits of those years and building upon them.

Science, research and intuitive minds have helped to create this era of ageless thinking. Computer technology stimulates the brain to better reasoning and analysis. More information is available about the proper care and treatment of the body. For example, from 17 to 25 vitamins and minerals can be found in tablets and health drinks. They help to build an efficient body. We all know this is furthered through exercise, sports, games, team play, walking – to mention only a few of the opportunities for physical activity. All offer new possibilities for rejuvenation after 50.

Keeping the body active – as it was born to be – contributes to good living and more energy. We can look nifty after fifty. We don't need to look like Whistler's mother or maybe our grandmothers who thought there was no alternative to decline. We can be as attractive and stylish as our younger sisters. Women are doing it! Life can be continuous fulfillment and pleasure if we put thought and energy into making it happen.

This book offers you the challenge to "grow young." Books in the bibliography add inspiration and motivation to this new trend in world history. I enthusiastically recommend them. They have helped me to realize that "growing young" is indeed practical, but it is a spiritual quest as much as it is a healthy and happy adventure.

Jo Paddicord

CHAPTER I

Attitude – Thinking, Planning and Chuckles Make Good Things Happen

If you want the rainbow,
you gotta put up with the rain.
– Dolly Parton

Attitude is the way we see ourselves and the world. Life goes forward, backward or coasts in neutral. Attitude reflects our thinking. When it is creative and coupled with planning, change is more graciously acceptable. Becoming a strong thinker and planner, we can sail through the downturns. To become strong involves being alert to what passes through the mind. Throwing out depressing, defeatist, negative thoughts and opening up to corrective, affirmative, and constructive ones is not always easy. Negative and positive choices take the same effort. One leads to depression, the other to harmony and peace of mind. Peace of mind comes when we recognize the bad stuff, deal with it, then let it go.

Getting bogged down in distressing news that is continually broadcast in print, television and radio will not help us "grow young." Constant complaining and obsession with bad news obscure hope. The better way is to analyze what is happening in your world with good common sense, and get on with living on the sunny side.

Controlling thoughts is an exercise in stick-to-itiveness. This challenge involves energizing thoughts that contribute to harmony and tossing out whatever nourishes pessimism.

Opening our lives to creative endeavors channels our thinking into positive directions and achievements. Creativity in its infinite aspects is a loving force, present in everyone, that develops in us the power to overcome difficulties. The more creative we are the more powerful we become. Ultimately, we realize the sun is always shining behind the clouds.

Cloudy thinking is a signal to make adjustments. Dr. Gerald Jampolsky, in his book *Teach Only Love*, says we will not be at peace as long as we think of ourselves as vulnerable to growing old and feeble, or if we focus on a miserable self-image, which blocks recognition of the person we really are. He suggests changing our perception – *think only what makes us truly happy to think* and get back to our original assignment, namely, to learn and teach love. That includes loving the goodness in ourselves and in everyone. Mother Teresa, renowned religious leader and a Nobel peace prize recipient who worked with lepers and the poorest of the poor, says in her book, *No Greater Love* that loving must be as normal to us as living and breathing...day after day, bestowed on those who are near and those afar.

Great thinkers, past and present, have often said the same in different words. We need reminders to keep us on track with ideas that beget good living. Planning our thinking and thinking our plan enables us to stay on the sunny side.

Don't retire! A couple of years before a friend retired from her job in the corporate world, she decided that to be content with retirement, she had to figure out a routine. She started planning a new career that followed her interest and study of many years. Evenings and weekends, she detailed and wrote down her plans – where she would get clients, her range of service, accounting procedures and consultants. While blueprinting her new venture, excitement welled up as she realized the potential. When retirement came, she plunged in with enthusiasm and anticipation. After a few years, she had as much business as she could handle. Before retirement, she had accumulated knowledge, worked her new business in her spare time and laid the foundation. After "retirement" she had new purpose.

George Burns wrote in his book, *How to Live to Be a 100 or More*, that if you're thinking about retiring, don't. Retiring from serving, working, learning – life-giving activities – starts a downhill slide. Unconsciously, we start to practice being old by adopting smaller steps, poor posture, sloppy looks and lazy thinking. One retiree went into an employment office for seniors. After reviewing her resumé, the consultant looked at her and said, "I can only pay you $7.95 an hour." The woman replied, "That's okay. I have to work. I'll take whatever you've got!" She was glad to have the job even though it paid so little relative to her experience.

Most work is a form of service. It seems like play when we enjoy it. If work for hire is not in the picture, enrich life by adopting a simple rule: Always have something to look forward to. Reposition your life to include variety – work/service, play, maintenance and personal time. Maintenance includes eating healthy, staying fit and improving appearance. Each of these directly influences attitude and are the subjects of chapters two, three and four. During personal time or introspection, we sort through thoughts and plans. Planning forces us to stay involved – to create a life we are happy living. When thinking stays on the creative track, boredom disappears.

Break through the barriers. Tuning up our thinking connects us to peace of mind and good health. One place to start is getting rid of the "can'ts" that hold us back. Changing from "can't" to "can do" is retreading our thinking wheels to roll from sad to glad, from afraid to trust, from impossible to probable. Solutions come more often with the can-do attitude. It requires determination, the kind used by disabled athletes. The Wheelchair Tennis Association, sponsored by the U.S. Tennis Association, has members who can outplay some walking opponents. The National Sports Center for the Disabled in Winter Park, Colo. teaches blind, one-legged and no-legged people to ski. They even participate in races down the snow-packed, sun-soaked mountain slopes. Encouraged by good instructors, they conquer their fears and feel the exhilaration of exceeding their limits. How sweet it is!

The media frequently broadcast true stories about people who triumph over disadvantages and break through mental and physical barriers.

Hearing about the accomplishments of our peers reminds us what the can-do attitude achieves. Women in their 50s, 60s, 70s, even 90s, are overcoming the limitations of age by staying fit through a planned physical activity routine, such as weight lifting, walking, yoga, t'ai chi, skiing, golf, baseball, and water exercises. One woman began learning to play tennis in her 60s. In two years she was the best player on a Gates Tennis Club competitive ladder in Denver, Colo. Now in her 70s, she is still competing. Marion Hart, sportswoman and author, learned to fly at 54, and made seven nonstop flights across the Atlantic. She was 83 on her last one. A four-foot ten-inch grandmother, Audrey Nobbe, won Outstanding Lifter Award at the NASA World Cup Powerlifting Championships in 1996 when she was 72.

With ingenuity and perseverance, women over 50 are increasing their income. Ann Wilder, 65, president of Vanns Spices in Towson, Md. has no intention of retiring from the company she founded in 1982. Virginia Adair, 83, who lives in a nursing home, published the fourth printing of her book of poetry in 1997 when publication of poetry was almost impossible. Edith Handy, 74, has been a waitress in a family restaurant in Grand Rapids, Mich. for 50 years, loves it and has no plans to quit. At 91, Lois Mailou Jones, a lifetime artist, exhibited her vibrant watercolors and sketches in the Bill Hodges Gallery, New York City – one of many exhibits, but a milestone in her career. She is still a working artist in African, Caribbean and Black American themes despite arthritis and a massive heart attack several years ago.

When work is unnecessary, active women volunteer their talents to hospitals, nonprofit associations, government, libraries and countless other organizations. A woman in her late 60s wrote to me that "life is a ball." One reason was her volunteer work at a hospital, where among other services, she was the Easter bunny and Mrs. Santa. A big part of the fun was being a clown. Groucho Marx said a clown is like an aspirin, only it works twice as fast.

Developing a purpose, a talent, an ability, or a skill is a potent force. The can-do attitude is not new. Remember these seniors?

★ Einstein was over 70 when he died in a hospital, his bed covered with papers he was working on.

★ American folk artist Grandma Moses started painting when she was 76 because arthritis made it impossible for her to embroider. She had her first one-woman show four years later.

★ George Burns wrote several books after 65. When he was 83, he played "God" in a movie. In fact, he made two "God" movies.

★ Picasso was still in full production at 90.

★ Arthur Rubenstein gave a stunning performance in Carnegie Hall at 90.

★ Verdi composed *Ave Maria* at 85.

★ Martha Graham danced professionally until 75 and choreographed her 180th work at 85.

★ At 85 Coco Chanel was head of her fashion design firm.

★ At 65 Winston Churchill took on the largest job of the first half of this century – the defeat of Nazism. He wrote a *History of the English-speaking Peoples* when he was 83.

★ Michelangelo was carving the *Rondanini Pieta* six days before he died at 89.

★ Golda Meir was 71 when she became prime minister of Israel.

★ Pablo Casals was doing concert tours at 88.

★ At 81 Benjamin Franklin was the mediator responsible for the U.S. Constitution.

★ At 93, Norman Vincent Peale, author of *The Power of Positive Thinking,* was giving 100 speeches a year without notes or assistance. He was advised by a friend, "Live your life and forget your age." Billy Graham would probably say the same.

Like the TV bunny with the battery, people keep on keeping on.

Change rejuvenates and fans energy. Planning life so that play, work, volunteering, self-care and learning are in the picture gives us control. The age of the mossbacks is long gone. Change is good in spite of the stress. A planned physical activity routine overcomes stress. Walking one to two miles a day – or 15 to 20 minutes – three times a week is an easy and convenient way. It's a fact: The harder the challenge the more rewarding the results. We know that improving thinking and living habits creates a happier, healthier life, and neutralizes old age patterns.

It's not too late to get fit, go to college, change careers, learn a profession or musical instrument, paint pictures – whatever makes life fascinating. When change improves the status quo, go for it! Don't be like this woman: She thought she had spent too much time and money learning the legal profession to change when she found she didn't like the lawyer business. She dejectedly concluded, "I'm too old now to switch careers." She was 30! Nowadays, women may have as many as five different occupations in a lifetime. They find an intelligent, planned change is healthy, refreshing, satisfying, and sometimes more lucrative.

Resistance to change is typical of "old" thinking. That is why we have to be as alert to thoughts as bees are to flowers. Attitudes that suggest "old" ruts of thinking are:
• Never volunteers, understands, smiles or laughs; constantly upset, never playful.
• Impatient, uncaring, selfish, unduly emotional, manipulative.
• Hopeless, critical of everything and everyone, complaining.
• Narrow-minded, frequently angry, capable but acting incapable, impolite.
• Unreasonable fear, self-important, never has a good word.
• Knows all the answers, disrespectful.
• "You owe me this because I'm _____."
• "After all I did for them, the least they could do is..."
• "I'm too tired to do that..."

Most of these are rooted in depressed or self-centered thinking. They find a quick exit when we build respect for ourselves and give more thought to the welfare of others.

Youthful thinking – not related to age – can be described as:
• Self-empowered, positive, doesn't take self too seriously.
• Enthusiastic, helpful, understanding, listens caringly, encouraging, loving, reliable.
• Playful, always learning, noncomplaining, considerate, slow to anger.
• Mentally strong, open to new friends and ideas, sharing, open-minded.

- Interested and interesting, has faith, wise, supportive, volunteers, plans activities.
- Sees the lighter side, cheerful, has a sense of humor.
- Maintains an attractive appearance, not dowdy or outdated.
- Stays physically active as possible.

We eliminate "old" thinking when we realize:
- Little things are NOT always important.
- We don't have to be the way we always were.
- We can change at any age.
- We can be different whenever it's good for health and happiness.
- No, it's not okay to be upset whenever we want to!
- Calmness engenders understanding.
- Other people's opinions are not more important than yours.
- It's never too late to get physically fit.
- We do have lots of choices.
- There will not be more time to do the good stuff tomorrow, next week, etc. Do it now!
- Thinking and feeling young after 50 is the way it's supposed to be.

To get rid of mental junk, concentrate on one item for a week then go on to something else. Discouragement sets in when we try to do too much. Keep it uncomplicated. Digesting a little is better than taking a big bite. Small daily victories are best.

Discovering inner strength contributes to a good attitude. Women who have survived traumatic illness find strength they never knew they had. One facet of inner strength is retaining control and not surrendering it to anyone. "No" is a popular word with wise people. Self-respect, a strong influence on attitude, thrives when we refuse to be doormats for

anyone. This happens when we listen discerningly to opinions, decide what is best for us, speak out, and stay positive.

---

*The greater part of our happiness or
misery depends on our dispositions, and
not on our circumstances. We carry the
seeds of the one or the other about with
us in our minds wherever we go.*

– Martha Washington (1731-1802)

The Value of Silence. Life is filled with so much noise
that it is a relief to the body, mind and spirit to escape into a
tranquility we can create. During personal quiet time, we
develop self-respect. The calm mind is a keener environment
for making smart decisions. Inner feelings are easier to understand and problems analyzed when anxiety and agitation are
absent. The objective is to maintain a listening attitude while
resting the body and mind in stillness. Perfecting our listening
subtly benefits interpersonal relationships.

In silence, free of distractions and after your mind is tran-
quil, enjoy the calm or think about what is important to you
– solutions, inspiration, guidance, nothing negative. To solve
problems, dump them into the silence and wait for answers.
They may not come that instant. This process fertilizes the
soil of your mind for the desired seed to grow. You cannot
rush the sprouting of the seed. Keep watering it with more
quiet time, contemplation and the sunshine of faith. Limiting
or distressing thoughts are weeds and you know what to do
with them.

There are many different ways to do this. Here is a basic procedure:

1. You can do it any time, any place, sitting in a church, a park, a bus, plane, etc. When the body is too restless to sit quietly, do ten minutes of walking, running in place or the exercises described on page _, Chapter 3. The gentle and controlled movements of yoga and t'ai chi help to restore a sense of peace to mind and body.
2. Sit upright.
3. Close your eyes and empty your mind. Banish anxious thoughts.
4. Count breaths, example: inhale and exhale 1, inhale and exhale 2, etc. up to 30. Then, mentally repeat an affirmation and/or inspiring idea. Keep your thinking on this level.
5. Protect your thoughts. Shut out disturbing ones. Only let in positive ones. Concentrate on one word or uplifting thought.
6. Relax into the peace. Start with five or 10 minutes. Let the time increase naturally as it gets more comfortable.

When problems are screaming at you, this is not easy to do. At first, keep the time short until you can maintain control. Persistence will gradually enable you to increase the time and give you an inkling of tranquility that you can hold to.

This is the one time in the day to give your mind and emotions a rest from worry and anxiety. Benefits: The serenity de-tenses the face and relaxes facial lines, leads to self-discovery, calms the senses, increases concentration, clears and conditions the mind for greater creativity and development. Ideas and resources to improve the status quo will start to percolate during this quiet time if you persist.

Affirm the positive. Affirmations give hope and discipline. People who know the power of thought recommend them. Dwelling on past wrongs, jealousies, resentments, and sadness has no benefit and merely adds another wrinkle. It is easier to quiet negatives by affirming a relevant positive. Affirmations are short statements in positive mode and in the present, active tense. Repeating an affirmation ten to fifty times throughout a day gets it rooted in the subconscious where ideas for corrective action germinate. You can also repeat them at wakeup time in the morning, midday and before falling asleep at night. Saying them aloud makes them more forceful. The writings of enlightened thinkers and religious thought have dynamic ideas that make concise affirmations to meet your every need. Rather than rehash wrongs, resentments, and hurts, it is far more helpful to think or say an affirmation until peace and relief settle in. Affirmations have wisdom and anticipate good results.

As you repeat affirmations, digest the meaning. Their purpose is to energize the mind for progress. The next step is take action. Ideas for action come unexpectedly – often, but not exclusively, during meditative moments.

Here are examples of affirmations to help you make up your own:
Every day, in every way, I'm getting better and better.
(Émile Coué)
Every day, in every way, I'm getting stronger and stronger.
I am now free of all self-destructive criticism.
I now have unconditional warm regards for all persons at all times.
I now release all comparisons with myself and others.
I plan each day to be healthy, happy and active.
I have the understanding and capacity to forgive.
I can develop the intelligence and sharp mind to create a good life.

Forgiving is maturing. Although forgiveness may seem as impossible as stopping the wind or waves, it is part of self-care. Practically everyone over a period of 50 years accumulates angers and grudges that weigh like a stone on the soul and threaten a healthy, happy life. Forgiveness brings inner healing that gives freedom from rage. Sometimes big things seem easier to forgive than little things. Getting rid of it all takes practice.

But, you say, some things are unforgivable. As righteous as it may seem, that is a negative thought and not true. Negatives are loads we can refuse to carry. As you know, the worst offenses can be and have been forgiven. A World of Forgiveness newsletter, published by the International Forgiveness Institute, P.O. Box 6153, Madison WI 53716-0153, October 1997 issue, related how a mother and father forgave the murderers of their sons. Terry Anderson said he forgave the Lebanese for his cruel seven-year confinement. He felt truly free when he overcame the anger and resentment. Hatred, no matter how justified, harms and burdens the holder, not the wrongdoer. This newsletter is loaded with inspiration.

You who want peace can find it only by complete forgiveness.

– *A Course in Miracles*

The ways to forgive are individual, but the basics are: Commit to it. Observe how anger affects your life. See your offender as one who has strengths and weaknesses, joys and sorrows just as you do. Find a way to accept the pain without transferring it to another person or relationship. Speak to the injurer. Be honest and pray.

Forgiveness is not forgetting. It is remembering but letting go and moving on, a process beginning with the decision to forgive. When we judge accurately that we have been wronged, forgiving frees us from the burden of resentment and pain, and of bondage to the wrongdoer. We break their power over us and the cycle of violence and revenge. Healing does not happen instantly and reconciliation may never come. Even the lack of response from the other person or persons does not prevent the forgiver from being healed The act of forgiving is a strong indication of maturity and wisdom. It is a gift of healing and personal growth – liberty from the blight of bitterness and anger.

From his studies and research, Dean Ornish, M.D. has found that forgiving your enemies has longtime benefits to your heart. His book, *Stress, Diet, and Your Heart,* explains that meditation and visualization can eliminate destructive emotions and help the health of our heart. Forgiving others should be partnered with forgiving oneself of past transgressions in order to remove the discomfort of inner guilt.

We all have scars and wounds. Our mission is to transcend them. Some of the things to do that keep you on the right track are:

√ Concentrate and develop an updated image. See yourself as you want to be.

√ Don't listen to self-critical mental tapes! Correct, adjust, then forget. Don't sweat the small stuff!

√ Get rid of fears. Positive action defeats them. One purpose of love is to destroy fear.

√ Never stop learning. Stretch your mind.

√ Welcome new adventures, new friends, new life-improving ideas.

√ Refuse to buy into the old thinking of others.

√ Look for ways to give the best you have. Cultivate good friends. True self-love is unselfish.

√ Reward yourself when you take the right action.

√ Give yourself a gift during the holidays; plan something special.

√ Plan – daily, weekly, monthly, annually. Always have a meaningful or fun event on your calendar.

Chip away at the rocky blocks of "I can't","I won't","I'm afraid." Just do it! Every day, every minute, people are freeing themselves from limitations. You can, too. Visit your library or bookstore and explore whatever attracts your curiosity. Libraries have special programs on book discussions, computers, and the internet. They offer free instruction on how to use their computers and free access to the internet. Cruising the internet is entertaining, educational and informative. If you want to learn more about computers, community schools and colleges have adult education classes.

Every time we learn something new we exercise the brain. "Use it or lose it" is true. The more we use the brain, the sharper it becomes. Learning through computers is another way to broaden our horizon, research interests and stay up-to-date.

Come on, let's play! Have we forgotten how to play because we think we're too old? How wrong can we get? Play recharges a can-do, positive attitude. During a walk in the park I sat on a swing and started soaring into the blue. A grandfatherly man strolled by with his dog and said, "That looks like fun!" Someday there may be playgrounds for us bigger kids. Remember the broader swings that didn't pinch your butt? Wouldn't it be fun to go down one of those long slides with rolling humps? We used to sit on wax candy wrappers to go faster. Riding a merry-go-round, singing little songs, exploring a park or bike path, sipping a root beer float, bring bubbling joy.

Why not play more and rediscover the simple, inexpensive fun of it? Mature women now have their own softball teams and experience the whoop of hitting a homer or catching a fly – the adrenaline rush of winning. Losing isn't so bad either because they had such a good time. Playing sparks the winning attitude and a healthy life. It's not beneath our dignity – we're not too old – to draw with crayons, put together a model airplane or car, roast marshmallows, blow soap bubbles, fly a kite, or mold something out of clay. That is why grandchildren are wonderful! They help us to renew our acquaintance with youth and do the things we used to love. But, let's not wait for grandkids to have tons of fun.

Planning your day or week with play lightens and brightens. Playing outdoors gives the extra benefit of healthy sunshine. Reward yourself with play when you have worked hard. Smiling and laughing symbolize the sweetness of life. Play makes it happen and is conducive to growing and thinking young. It uplifts, strengthens, cheers, puts a sparkle in our eyes and a spring in our step.

Light up life with a smile! At the beginning of my makeup classes, the women are all rather glum as they look into their mirrors and see their "bare" faces. They get increasingly happier as they see each added color do its job to bring out their real beauty. At the end of the classes, they are smiling and joking because they are so pleased with the almost magical difference that lovely, well-placed colorings can make.

Some reasons people don't smile are: They are unhappy (with their appearance?), too busy, have low self-esteem, are self-centered, ill, don't understand it as a sharing thing, never learned how, or forgot. Some even think that the serious face expresses more credibility and prestige; in some instances, yes – but all the time?

The reasons for smiling are many. At the end of makeup classes, the women were definitely more attractive, and smiling doubled their beauty. A smile reflects the inner beauty we may forget is there. Have you ever seen how a sad or stern face lights up with a smile? Right away it seems kinder, friendlier, more accepting. When you smile, you brighten the day for yourself and the people you meet, improve mental well-being, empower yourself, and create positive chemical and electrical charges in the brain. A smile is a gift; give it often.

Sometimes we have to relearn smiling that came so naturally in younger years. This type of smile is not fake, artificial or manipulative. It comes from a sincere, well-wishing heart and a smiling mind.

A laugh a day keeps the doctor away. The next time you are having a bad time, find something to laugh about. Think about it: A year hence, what is bothering you now will be forgotten. You'll have something else to worry about! Rent or purchase video cassettes of Charlie Chaplin, Laurel and Hardy, Buster Keaton, your favorite contemporary comedian or funny movie. Look for laughs by reading literary humor, such as E. B. and Katherine White's *Subtreasury of American Humor* or Max Eastman's *The Enjoyment of Laughter.* Other well-known works are those by Robert Benchley, S. J. Perelman, James Thurber, Art Buchwald or Erma Bombeck. Bombeck is the author of several books including *If Life is a Bowl of Cherries – What am I doing in The Pits.*

Cartoons are another way to brainwash our mind with humor. Never pass up a cartoon! Cartoonist B. Kliban has a book titled *Never Eat Anything Bigger Than Your Head and*

Other Drawings. The library is a super source for tapes, books and magazines.

If a smile improves the electrical charges in the brain, imagine what a good laugh does! Norman Cousins in his book, *Anatomy of an Illness,* explains how he recovered from a crippling and supposedly irreversible disease. To cope with pain he added the medicine of laughter to the clinical care prescribed by his doctor. His nurse read to him from humor books and he watched comedic films. By monitoring his progress, he found that his body reacted favorably to the positive emotion of laughter. It had a salutary effect on body chemistry, reducing the inflammation in his joints.

Laughing stimulates certain hormones that release endorphins in the brain. They are known as natural pain killers and foster a sense of well-being. The resulting relaxation counters heart disease, high blood pressure and depression.

So, let's be good to ourselves and laugh at our foibles. We don't have to take ourselves and our mistakes too seriously. When we do, stress sets in and occasionally self-depreciation. We think more clearly when we lighten up, and laughter does lighten the heavy stuff. Humor is a big fact of life. We love comedians because humor lessens our cares and worries. Who doesn't love to laugh? After 50, most of us need it more. It improves attitude and outlook, lifts the facial lines, settles the nerves, relieves tension, dissipates stress. Yes, both body and mind react favorably to laughter.

Some people collect jokes. When they hear a good one, they quickly write it down. Concentrate on esteem-building humor, not self-degrading or demeaning quips. A really good joke tickles your funny button every time you think of it. Usually, you can fit one in with the line "that reminds me..." When I first began giving talks, I can't tell you how surprised and pleased I was when they laughed at my jokes. Getting laughs is sheer pleasure. Practice a joke, memorize even dramatize a little. This exercises the memory and consequently, the brain. Discover the joy of bringing chuckles to your friends, but don't forget the punch line! On second thought, they may laugh at that more than the joke! You might want to read Steve Allen's *How to Be Funny: Discovering the Comic You*, one of the 41 books he has written. It has jokes you can use. They are in the public domain. Tailor them to suit your style.

Keep your dreams alive! They are the starry stuff that life is made of and one of the secrets to successful living. These are wonderful years because of the innumerable opportunities for fulfillment, adventure, and the modern perspective about longevity and lifestyle.

Attitude is everything. A good one teaches us that life is more than work, worry, illness and bills. Life is discovering and developing ourselves and extending our horizons. This is a time for enjoying beauty in all its aspects, a time for renewal and expanding the mind. It's a time to explore, make new friends, do new things, see new places, and to enjoy tranquility. It is our personal responsibility to be receptive to new directions and opportunities. Why not pursue the quest of our spirit and strive for the joys in life? We have the power to surmount negativity and cruise above it in the glorious spheres of creativity, appreciation, truth, and faith.

CHAPTER 2

Eat Healthy and Enjoy the Sunshine of Life

> *Just remember that you can't fool your body, but you can certainly <u>fuel</u> it. Fill it up on low-fat, nutritious, healthy foods. Your stomach will think you're one smart cookie.*
> *– Looneyspoons, Low-Fat Food Made Fun by Janet & Greta Podleski*

Color on your plate is as important as color on your face and figure. Oranges, red apples and tomatoes, yellow bananas, orange sweet potatoes, green beans and peas – to mention a few – all fuel your body, keeping it vital, primed for good health and its full potential. When your meal is pleasing to the eye, it will keep you well.

What follows is a basic nutrition guide for women over fifty and is not intended to cover the complexities of nutrition. Hundreds of books and magazines do that. The partner to eating healthy is staying fit (chapter 3). Planned physical activity stimulates the circulation and absorption of nutrients throughout the body so they can do their maintenance job. This dual action – physical activity and healthy eating – also energizes the brain, keeping us mentally alert. Life is one hundred times more satisfying.

As far back as Hippocrates in ancient Greece, philosphers and physicians taught that eating the right foods would prevent and cure disease. But, only recently have scientific tests and studies begun to prove this. For example, a scientific test reported in Harvard Women's Health Watch newsletter (April 1998) showed that a low-fat, dairy-rich diet abounding in fruits and vegetables could be as effective as drugs in bringing borderline hypertension back to the normal range. In addition, the nutrients in green, orange, yellow and red plant foods are regarded as increasingly important to the prevention of some cancers and diseases. Substances found in berries, cherries, raisins and tomatoes can help eliminate blood clots that cause heart attacks.

Bad habits interfere with the body's innate powers of recuperation and rejuvenation, but good eating habits reinforce the body's built-in defense system. A healthy diet for us is twofold: Eat plant foods and supplements.

Plant foods. The most effective sources are a variety of fruits and vegetables, particularly leafy greens and red-pigmented foods. Nutrition experts and researchers universally agree on the importance of chomping of fruits and vegetables – uncooked whenever possible, so that none of their nutritional value is lost. They are also cholesterol-free. Variety is important because it is assurance that we will get all the nutrients and other substances needed for a lifetime of good health and lower cancer risk. Mounting evidence suggests that foods are preferable to supplements because they contain antioxidants and micronutrients that act synergistically in the body, making it less likely to develop cancers, heart disease or cataracts.

Supplements, a multivitamin/mineral tablet or liquid supplement. Nutritional supplements are available as capsules or tablets, or as beverage, such as Ensure, and are formulated to provide a concentrated form of nutrients. They are not substitutes for a healthy diet and cannot make up for a poor diet. When you think your diet may have specific nutritional shortfalls, a standard multivitamin and mineral tablet taken daily makes sense. When you are pressed for time, drink a liquid nutritional supplement rather than skip a meal. For all nutrients, usually, 100 percent of the Required Daily Allowance (RDA) is all we need. This information is listed on the containers. Taking too much of a supplement can reverse the benefits.

How are nutrients measured? The energy in foods is measured by calories. Proteins, fats, carbohydrates (starches and sugars), and fibers are measured in grams (g). Grams are small units, for example: 28.33 grams equals one ounce.

Calcium, iron, vitamins C and E, and other vitamins and minerals are measured in milligrams (mg) – one-thousandth of a gram and micrograms (mcg) – one millionths of a gram.

Vitamins A, D, and sometimes E are measured in international units (IUs), which are roughly equivalent to milligrams (mgs). Vitamin A may also be measured in *retinol equivalents* (RE). One IU of vitamin A equals 0.3 RE. You can see it takes a small amount to obtain nutritional benefits.

As you know, too much of a good thing is not that good. Megadoses of vitamins or minerals cause an imbalance. This is particularly true of A, D, E and K because they are stored in the body and large doses can be toxic. For example, too much vitamin D can actually cause bone loss and too much calcium may cause kidney stones. Note: Without K, blood would not clot.

Ads for supplements with antioxidants give them the aura of "miracle workers," but this is seldom the case. Not all supplements have the combinations that contribute the most benefits. A supplement may contain sugar, which is not good for high blood pressure. Choose one that is about 100 percent of the RDA for vitamins and minerals. Check the expiration date. Supplements lose their potency if too old. High-priced brands are often no better than store or generic brands. You might want to talk to the manager in a health food store or someone who really knows the products. Describe what you want and they will give you helpful advice.

Fiber. PILLS ARE NOT MAGIC BULLETS! Research has not yet proved that supplements prevent diseases as effectively as the nutrients in natural foods. Capsules and liquid supplements do not always contain fiber and other nutrients necessary for a healthy body. You still need the riches of fiber. Why? Because it plays a role in preventing colon cancer and constipation, reduces the risk of heart problems, keeps blood glucose (sugar) levels in check, and promotes weight loss.

Some food sources for fiber are: Cereals with wheat, bran and oatmeal, whole grains, barley, brown rice, macaroni, spaghetti, Bartlett pears, oranges, stewed prunes, peas, beans, asparagus, frozen corn, almonds with skins, skins of fruits and vegetables.

ANTIOXIDANT ALL STARS, A DISEASE-FIGHTING ARSENAL
What they are, what they do and where they are found

The fact that we are living longer has increased the awareness of the health-giving benefits of antioxidants. They have been around since plants sprouted and are plentiful in foods. Some antioxidants are manufactured by the cells in our body and are called enzymes. They protect against excess oxidation. Oxidation occurs when body cells use oxygen for energy and the destruction of infectious invaders. When there is too much oxidation, some electrons in the cells become destabilized and damaged and turn into free radicals. These are the rascals that cause disease and wrinkles. The same process makes sliced apples brown and metals rust. As in apples and metals, external factors – such as air pollution, carbon monoxide, pesticides, cigarette smoke, the radiation found in ultraviolet light and X rays – can also cause free radicals in the human body.

Cigarette smoke depletes the body's store of vitamin C – a strong antioxidant – and is a major source of free radicals. If you smoke or work around smokers, eat more antioxidant-rich foods and take daily supplements of vitamins C and E. These vitamins and other antioxidants help to inactivate the compounds that cause aging, cancer and heart disease.

Cells have ways of fighting bad agents and repairing themselves. The body produces antioxidants. Research has discovered they slow the aging process, prevent diseases and brain damage by destroying excessive oxidation. One of the most powerful is glutathione. There is a wonderful connection and cooperation among the trillions of cells in all parts of the body. Ingesting foods and supplements rich in antioxidants reinforces them to fight free radicals. Eating antioxidant foods keeps us youthful, active, and healthier than if we do not.

Research is ongoing regarding the protection of antioxidants against arthritis, Parkinson's disease and diabetic retinopathy (which can lead to blindness). After 50 it is even more important for us to avoid a deficiency in antioxidants.

The big antioxidants are vitamins A, C, E, melatonin and carotenoids. To make it easier for you, some, but not all, food sources are given for each antioxidant.

Vitamin A: It enhances the white blood cell function, improves resistance to infection and carcinogens, and is crucial for your immune defense.

Food sources: Organ meats, fish, cod liver oil, eggs, milk fortified with A, dark green, orange and red fruits and vegetables, sweet potatoes, tuna. The body converts foods rich in beta carotene into vitamin A.

Beta Carotene: It is a form of vitamin A and one of more than 600 carotenoids. Carotinoids are found in yellow, red, orange and deep green fruits and vegetables. Many are thought to protect against disease and some forms of cancer. Beta carotene plays an important role in the maintenance of skin, teeth, nails, hair, eyes and bones. It protects the eyes from cataracts by preventing the oxidation of the lens, stimulates immunity, cuts the risk of cancers in the colon and respiratory system, and the risk of heart disease. Studies suggest it will have an adverse effect if taken as a supplement by a smoker.

Food sources: Yellow, orange, red fruits and vegetables, dark green vegetables, broccoli, cabbage, asparagus, carrots, cantaloupe, peaches, apricots, pink grapefruit, tomatoes, sweet potatoes. Corn contains lutein, an antioxidant and carotenoid. When combined with dark green vegetables, it may help prevent age-related blindness and damage to eyes from sunlight.

Vitamin C: An immune system booster *par excellence*, it is essential to the maintenance of the body's vital organ systems – respiration, circulation, and vision. It is the most prevalent and critical antioxidant in our lungs, protecting them, relieving asthma, and decreasing bronchial problems. (Onions have quercetin, another natural antioxidant and antihistamine that benefits asthmatics.) Vitamin C has antihistamine properties that fight allergic reactions, cold symptoms and infections. Taking extra vitamin C lowers blood pressure, creates healthier cholesterol levels, reduces risk of heart disease and cancer. When you are under stress, take additional vitamin C. Five servings of fruits and vegetables daily supplies more than 200 mg. Daily recommendation: 60-500 mg.

Food sources: Guavas, green peppers, broccoli, kale, raw cabbage, cantaloupes, orange juice, apple juice and other citrus juices, juices fortified with C, strawberries, kale, navel oranges, tomatoes, tomato juice.

Vitamin E: A survey of older Americans showed that 40 percent have low intakes of this vitamin because it is not plentiful in foods. Those who take 400 to 800 IUs of vitamin E daily have a significant reduction in infections and 75 percent had less chance of cardiovascular problems. Buy vitamin E labeled "mixed tocopherols," rather than plain vitamin E. Vitamins C and E help maintain healthy levels of nitric oxide, a chemical that widens blood vessels. E also helps to reduce muscle damage and soreness caused by exercise and may even slow the course of Alzheimer's. E protects against cell damage, encourages cell growth and recovery from oxidative damage including brain tissue, increases antioxidant enzyme activity and protects other antioxidants, such as vitamins A and C. Excessive amounts are not better.

Food sources: Beets, black beans, broccoli, sunflower and other seeds, almonds and peanuts, sardines, corn and safflower oil, green leafy vegetables, sweet potatoes, whole grains cereals, tomato juice.

Selenium: It is an essential trace mineral and part of the enzyme glutathione. As an antioxidant enzyme, it works with vitamin E to fight cell damage and assist in the formation of antioxidant enzymes. Selenium supplements can lower the risk of various forms of cancer but the best source is food. Selenium plus healthy doses of vitamins C, E, and carotenoids lowers the risk of allergic reactions, eases breathing by restricting the action of free radicals in the lungs and in parts of the cardiovascular system. Excess is harmful and toxic, 200 mcg/day is recommended.

Food sources: Fish and seafood, lean red meat, brazil nuts, sunflower seeds, turkey dark meat, chicken breast, brown and white rice, oatmeal, whole-grain cereals and breads.

Zinc: It is essential in healing wounds and sores, restores flagging immunity and, with selenium, helps mental performance. Zinc is essential for normal tissue renewal and skeletal development. Daily recommendation is 15 mg and may be doubled to strengthen immunity.

Food sources: Oysters, crab, shrimp, lamb, beans with tomato sauce, legumes (peas and beans), nuts, sardines, organ meats, dark chicken meat, whole-grain cerals and breads.

Lycopene: It is a carotenoid and scavenges free radicals more effectively than vitamins C and E. Lycopene is one of many plant pigments with antioxidant properties and gives plants their yellow, orange and red colors. Bright red colors spell richness in lycopene. Benefits are: reduces the risk of heart disease; protects against cervical and digestive tract cancers, age-related damage to the eyes, and sun damage to the skin.

Food sources: Tomatoes and all their products. Processed tomatoes are just as potent as fresh ones. In fact, the processing of tomatoes increases the bioavailability of lycopene. Research is showing this nutrient should be part of our daily ritual.

Flavonoids: They have antioxidant properties and prevent free radicals, inhibit the destruction of the lipids in cell membranes, fight cancer, and protect vitamins A, D and E.

Food sources: Yellow, red and orange fruits.

Melatonin: Just as adrenaline is produced by the adrenal glands, melatonin is a hormone produced by the pineal gland

and pumped through the blood stream. This process occurs during the night or dark periods of the day. Regular sleep patterns are important to the body's biological clock because they stimulate the production of melatonin. Melatonin is related to the skin pigment melanin, hence its name. Being the strongest antioxidant, it is the most efficient scavenger of free radicals, followed by vitamin E. Melatonin acts within cells to protect DNA from free radical damage. It controls the aging process by protecting the body's immune systems, reducing blood clotting a defense against heart attacks, stroke and many other diseases, and fights free radicals in the brain. Air travelers can avoid jet lag by taking a melatonin supplement. As one of many hormones, it regulates body processes, such as digestion, menstruation, circulation and sleep. It is nontoxic and has no known lethal dose.

Food sources: Dairy products, cheese, milk, poultry (especially turkey), eggs, tuna. All of the food sources mentioned for vitamins and minerals facillitate the manufacture of melatonin.

EXTRA TIPS ABOUT VITAMINS AND MINERALS

Scientists are discovering more about the connection between good health and vitamins and minerals. According to surveys, Americans do not consume enough of the key vitamins and minerals: Vitamins C, D, B-6, B-12, folacin (a B vitamin), zinc, magnesium and calcium.

Vitamins B-6 and B-12 offer benefits regarding asthma and heart disease, and help to maintain a healthy skin and sound nervous system. B-12 helps to prevent anemia. According to the National Academy of Sciences (May 1999), people over 50 should take a B-12 supplement. The ability to absorb this vitamin from food sources decreases with age.

Food sources of B-6: Fish, poultry, organ meats, bananas, avocados, sunflower seeds, sweet potatoes, whole brown rice, legumes, milk. Daily recommendation: 1.6 mg.

Food sources of B-12: Eggs, meats, poultry, fish, shellfish, yogurt, cottage cheese, cereals fortified with B-12. Daily recommendation: 2.4 mcg.

Vitamin D: It is essential for calcium absorption that builds healthy bone. The body manufactures D when sunlight hits the skin. D. After 50 the skin gradually creates less vitamin D from sunshine. One way to get it is with a daily multivitamin. (Harvard Women's Health Watch 1/98) Studies show that at least one-third of elderly people who have hip fractures are deficient in D. A daily diet rich in vitamin D reduces this risk. Daily recommendation: between 50 and 70, 400 IUs; after 70, 600 IUs. Some experts recommend more calcium and D to prevent osteoporosis.

Food sources: Milk fortified with D, cod liver oil, salmon, tuna, eggs, cheddar cheese, some cereals that are fortified with it.

Calcium: It is the primary mineral for strong bones and is especially important if you are on estrogen. The absorption of calcium by the body is boosted by the vitamin D found in sunshine. This means less susceptibility to fractures caused by bone-thinning osteoporosis. The combination of calcium and vitamin D plus an exercise program slows the loss of bone mass, preventing or postponing osteoporosis. Women over 50 and 60 need calcium supplements, taken at meals, to get the daily recommended 1300 to 1500 mg; 2500 is too much.

Food sources: Milk, yogurt, cheddar cheese, lowfat cottage cheese, kale, Swiss chard, greens, almonds, sardines, salmon, firm tofu, calcium-fortified orange juice.

Magnesium: It is important to bone formation, fights osteoporosis, works in over 300 physical functions, lower blood pressure, keeps heart heathy, eliminates brain fog, helps to relax muscles; 1000 mg daily has been found to help asthmatics. A deficiency increases the risk of confusion and depression. Normal daily intake is 320 mg.

Food sources: Tofu, whole grains, oatmeal, almonds and cashews, seeds, legumes, green leafy vegetables, potato, salmon and semisweet chocolate chips (surprise!)

THE ANTI-AGING DIET

Keep your diet simple because overeating strains the heart-pump. A diet low in fat and high in fruits, vegetables and dairy products reduces blood pressure. Add fiber and you have an all-purpose eating plan. Low fat doesn't mean no fat. A teaspoon of margarine or butter, or some milk or yogurt makes it possible for vitamins and minerals to be fully absorbed for optimum health. Body linings, the skin and complexion need essential fatty acids (EFAs) to prevent parching, cracking, and scaling.

Skin problems may occur with a Spartan, low-fat diet. Skin and hair needs fluids, vitamins, minerals, and some fats to rebuild and stay moist. Poor nutrition affects everything from neurological functioning to muscle strength and increases the risk of infections and chronic diseases. Major minerals for us are zinc, magnesium and calcium. Most of us need to eat more fruits and vegetables to get enough vitamins C and E.

YOUR GUIDE FOR EATING HEALTHY

- Plenty of fruits, especially oranges, cantaloupe, cherries, berries, tomatoes and vegetables. Get variety by including broccoli, sweet potatoes, squash, carrots and green leafy vegetables. Daily recommendation: two fruits, three vegetables.

Tip: Steamed or microwaved vegetables
retain more vitamins.

- Fiber-rich whole grains such as 100 percent whole wheat bread, oatmeal, bran cereals and brown rice.

The above two items will give you most of the vitamins, minerals and nutrients your body needs.

- Little fat. Canola and olive oil have unsaturated fats that may protect against cancer and heart disease.
- Limit red meat. Substitute beans, fish (twice a week is a good idea), lamb and chicken. Remove skin from poultry, because that's where the saturated fat is.
- Take a multivitamin supplement or health drink that provides essential minerals and anti-aging vitamins.
- Skim or 1% fat milk or low-fat yogurt, cheese, nuts and seeds.
- Take extra vitamin C, E and calcium, when required. For women over 50, 250-500 mg of vitamin C and 200-800 IU of vitamin E *beyond the RDAs* are recommended because of their antioxidant protection.

A WORD ABOUT CITRUS FRUITS

Citrus fruits have been used for thousands of years as natural remedies for a variety of ailments. Besides having vitamin C, they also supply carotenoids. Some specific benefits are:

Kumquat juice to clear up bronchitis

Lemon juice with a pinch of table salt to soothe a sore throat

Lime juice in warm water to help the aches and cramps from
flu

Tangerine juice to break up mucous congestion in the lungs
Papaya juice to aid digestion
  (See *Encyclopedia of Healing Juices* by Robert Heinerman)

  I drink a breakfast cocktail that has prevented flu and its relatives – without shots – for years. When I say it contains cod liver oil, women cringe and shudder. BUT, I use *flavored* cod liver oil – orange, cherry, or mint. Health food stores and super markets have it. One teaspoon of Dale Alexander's Norwegian Cod Liver Oil provides 4600 IUs of vitamin A and 460 IUs of vitamin D. Blend the following:

  1 teaspoon cod liver oil
  1/2 banana
  6 ounces of orange juice or milk (Orange juice and sunlight enhance your ability to fight free radicals.)

WHAT ABOUT EGGS?

  One little egg is an energizing pack of all nutrients except vitamin C with a small amount of saturated fat. So, they may be okay for some people. The yolk has lots of cholesterol, about 215 milligrams, more than two-thirds of the recommended daily intake of 300mg. The whites are pure protein with a little riboflavin and potassium. Many factors determine cholesterol levels and their impact on heart disease risk. For some of us, adding or subtracting an egg from the daily diet would have no big effect on blood cholesterol, especially if your daily meals are typically an egg for breakfast, a vegetarian lunch and dinner with little or no meat.

  The American Heart Association advises that if cholesterol is at a desirable level, you can eat up to four eggs a week. On the other hand, if you are trying to reduce your blood cholesterol level and high blood pressure or have a family history of heart disease, one egg a week may be enough.

Tip: In recipes, replace one whole egg with one-quarter cup egg substitute or two egg whites.

GRAZING IS GREAT!

Help prevent weight gain and make eating easier with several small meals a day instead of two to three larger ones. Space your eating times according to your preferred schedule. You can get more control over your weight and hunger and increase your quality of sleep and energy. A mini-meal guideline for one day is:

A bowl of cereal and sliced banana or berries with milk
Fruit or vegie juice and a peanut butter or turkey sandwich on whole wheat bread
Spaghetti and a tossed salad
One liquid supplement with a bran muffin.

Some women like their bigger meal midday. When they eat out, they ask for a half-order or share an entree. When you feel like munching, think about raw carrots, cabbage, celery, apples, pop corn, or nuts. Eating less and better can be best.

SECRETS TO KEEPING OFF THE POUNDS

Successful dieters aren't just lucky. They strive to lose pounds for health and appearance reasons. A study by James Hill, a nutritionist at the University of Colorado-Denver and Rena Wing, a psychologist at the University of Pittsburgh, revealed key facts to achieving the shape you want.

Do it for yourself! Change your attitude and realize the motivation to do it starts with you, no one else.

Get real and set short-term goals. Plan to lose five pounds in two weeks instead of 40 pounds in six months.

Do not deprive yourself of favorite foods. Instead take smaller portions and allow for some indulgence. Be good to yourself!

Watch fat intake. Gram for gram, fat has more than twice the calories of carbohydrates and some women store fat cells better than they burn them.

Exercise regularly. Make it a routine. It doesn't necessarily matter how long (30 minutes is best) but that you do it every day. Losing pounds is a sure thing when you faithfully observe this one. Women who stick with a fitness program at least three times a week seldom overeat.

Track your routine. Self-monitoring is a predictor of success because it shows determination. Writing it down is like marking your mind. Record your weight, food intake and time spent for daily exercise. Every day write something good about YOU.

Become a good organizer and problem solver. Plan your time to include exercise, shopping, menus, work and play. Manage your day and develop problem solving skills.

Adopt a plan for life. Understand the emotions involved with lifestyle changes to attain your goal. The "honeymoon" state is optimistic and usually fades. The "frustration" stage may last for months, even years. You may feel angry when you realize how hard you have to work to lose and keep off weight. The "tentative acceptance" stage sets in when you move from understanding, to fully implementing, to actually living your resolve. Once you get here, there is no turning back! You're on the way to getting the gold. Congratulations!

Pounds stay off only if you combine healthy eating with a fitness program forever. One without the other will not do the job.

Getting rid of the cellulite look
involves the same process as
reducing fat anywhere else on the body:
cutting back on the fat you eat and
getting some regular exercise.

Looneyspoons, Low-fat Food Made Fun

WATER

As years roll by, our ability to sense thirst decreases. Consequently, we should not wait until we are thirsty before drinking water. Never pass up a water fountain! Evian water is bottled in plastic containers with 11 oz of spring water. One easily fits into your purse or athletic bag so you can have a drink wherever you are and especially when you are physically active.

Some of our water needs are supplied by fruits – especially watermelons and cantaloupes – vegetables and their unsweetened and unsalted juices. The water in food and beverages counts, too. But, concentrated alcoholic beverages, such as vodka, brandy, and some caffeinated beverages increase urine production, leading to loss of water and possible dehydration. Your body retains half the fluid from coffee, tea and colas. This equates to eight ounces of water for every 16 oz. of a caffeinated drink. Milk is more a food than a drink but it has lots of water. If you dislike water, like so many things in life, "get over it."

Ninety percent of the body is water, and yet, it is recognized as "the forgotten nutrient." We overlook its life-giving benefits. It helps the body transport nutrients, aids digestion, removes wastes, prevents urinary tract infections and constipation, regulates body temperature and weight, and lubricates all cell processes and organ functions.

Water is lost through sweat and urine and most of us do not relace it. Losing water through perspiration can cause fatigue and lower performance. When necessary, gradually increase your water intake but avoid overloading your bladder. Start with a big glass in the morning. Drink most of the recommended daily consumption in the mornings and afternoons. For a tart twist, add flavoring pineapple, lemon, orange, kiwi or cranberry juice.

How do you know if you are getting enough water? Notice the color of your urine. When you urine is usually light yellow, you're drinking enough. When it is dark, increase your intake.

BRAIN POWER

Scientists call the brain the three pound universe. Did you know that it deteriorates because it is flesh and blood? But, like any flesh-and-blood organ, the right maintenance, rejuvenation and stimulation enable it to function properly throughout our entire life, according to *The New England Journal of Medicine*.

One of the keys to healthy brains is antioxidant nutrients. They fight the free radicals that cause tumors and physical changes associated with aging. Vitamins C, E and the carotenoids protect the arteries to the brain and safeguard the brain itself. Vitamin B12 (not found in plant foods) and folic acid, found in beans, peas, oranges, green vegetables and whole grains, help to deliver oxygen to the brain and improve concentration. When your diet is short of these foods, a multivitamin with folic acid will be helpful.

Fish is brain food. It contains a polyunsaturated fat that is the most abundant fat in your brain. Other brain foods are essential fatty acids, nuts, seeds, vegetable oils, synthetic sources of B6 and B12, dairy, meats, vitamins C, E and carotenoids.

Some causes of memory loss are lack of physical and mental exercise, overeating, overdrinking alcohol, and stress. Creating good habits eventually neutralizes the bad ones. You can stimulate brain power by reading a book, doing memory exercises and crossword puzzles, participating in interesting conversations, learning new skills or reviving an old one. Examples: learn a musical instrument or foreign language, paint, draw, write or plan a trip. The concentration during all sports and exercise also exercises the brain. Richard Leviton's book *Brain Builders* is about maintaining age-proof mind power. He gives 36 exercises (he calls them workouts) to wake up your hidden mental resources as well as foods and antioxidants to feed the brain.

Design the eating program that suits your appetite and taste preferences. To get the right balance between foods and supplements, you may wish to confer with a registered dietitian. The names of those in your area may be obtained by calling the American Dietetic Association at 800-366-1655. Website http:www.eatright.org.

When right living and a balanced diet are maintained, the body's own life energy "electrocutes" diseases. Eating should be a pleasant experience and fuel the enjoyment of a life free from limiting health problems. We can grow young and enjoy life by cultivating a strong body and mind with life-giving eating habits.

*"Instead of assisting me,
see if you can get some swing music on the sound system."*

CHAPTER 3

Stay Fit to Get Joy Out of Every Day

"We know people who died at 40 and were buried at 70....God didn't set any age at which we have to slow down, so don't do it!...Do something. Do anything! Get off your butt!"
– Jack LaLanne, America's godfather of fitness and good health*

Staying fit makes all facets of life happier. It enables us to sleep better, kiss the blues goodbye and be physically and mentally strong. Reports from the U.S. Surgeon General, The American Heart Association and The American College of Sports Medicine affirm that deconditioning more than years is the cause of problems associated with aging. The older we get the more we need regular exercise. An exercise routine helps the body to repair, maintain and improve itself and can prevent and treat disease.

We can be frisky after fifty! Moderate fitness activity, such as the exercises given in this chapter, benefits body and mind. Add to this walking, a sport, aquacize, dancing, something you enjoy and you have the recipe for growing young. Physically active people have a greater work capacity and stamina than their inactive peers. Fitness enables you to look like the vital person you are. You have more freedom, confidence and it's a great connector. You meet new people and stay

*From an article by photo journalist Dee Dunheim in *The Senior News*, Dundee, IL

involved. Life is more satisfying once you decide upon a planned, lifelong fitness program.

"I hate exercise!" Don't call it exercise. Call it doing yourself a favor! Jack LaLanne hates exercise but he works out vigorously every day at his home in Central California. Changing mindsets is a big obstacle because change is not easy. The enemies to exercise are apathy, depression and inertia. These are the very attitudes that planned physical activity eliminates. If you resist exercise of any kind and have been sedentary, start to challenge your mind by reading everything in newspapers, magazines and books on exercise and sports. Clip articles for rereading. Saturate your mind with information to spur your will to adopt this element of a rewarding lifestyle.

Staying physically fit and eating healthy are matters of self-preservation so that we can have a happy, rewarding and useful life. Visit a recreation center and notice the energy and reactions of participants. Begin with short intervals of exercise five to ten minutes and gradually increase the time. Investigate t'ai chi. Take a class. Join a walking or biking club. Smart people do everything they can to make the years after 50 productive, healthy, and adventurous. If you are still unconvinced, visit a nursing home.

If exercise were a drug, it would be the
most prescribed pill in the world
(paraphrased from Robert Butler, the first
director of The Institute on Aging). It has
a powerful effect on extending and
improving the quality of life.

Do it now! When you don't take time for wellness, you will have to for illness. Planned fitness activity saves money on medical bills. A good workout eliminates the sluggish feeling with a rush of energy. Best of all, it's never too late to start. The body responds at any age.

No group in our population can benefit more from a fitness program than people over 50. Our muscles are just as responsive to weight lifting as those of younger people. Rest is exactly what we don't need. You've heard it said "when we rest, we rust." Well, that's no joke. Take it seriously. We don't have to be a competitive athlete to benefit from exercise.

Whenever you feel lazy and think, "tomorrow I'll do it" read over the following list and realize today is the time.

THE BENEFITS FROM PLANNED PHYSICAL ACTIVITY
That which is used develops; that which is not used wastes away.
                                              – Hippocrates

Reduces premature aging and slows down degeneration, decreases medical problems and medications.

Stimulates the flow of blood making the body more powerful, decreases the tendency for blood to pool in the legs and cause varicose veins.

Improves the flow of blood and oxygen to the brain, preserving short-term memory, increasing alertness and the ability to reason, and helps to tap into the brain's own natural tranquilizers.

Wards off heart disease and stroke by improving the cardiovascular system, helps to control high blood pressure, increases good HCL cholesterol and lung capacity.

Reduces the future risk of breast cancer when women are athletic, according to preliminary evidence.

Lessens anxiety, hypertension, boredom and mental fatigue; strengthens the body's ability to cope with stressful demands, lowering susceptibility to both mental and physical illness.

Builds stamina and endurance for daily activities by increasing resistance to fatigue.

Assuages grumpiness and loneliness, generates energy, optimism and creativity, fights life-paralyzing depression.

Improves the overall sense of wellbeing, adds vitality to appearance, a sense of joy, achievement, confidence, and competence.

Preserves youthful vigor, quality of life and a healthy outlook.

How long should we exercise? The Centers for Disease Control and Prevention recommend moderate exercise for at least 30 minutes most days of the week. To achieve weight loss, exercise every day for at least 30 minutes. For cardiovascular conditioning, spend a minimum of 20 minutes three to four times a week doing weight-bearing exercises. Weight-bearing exercises are done on your feet and include walking, running, stair-climbing, step aerobics, cross training, cycling and dancing.

Even strolls, walking at a moderate pace, and a simple, vigorous, ten-minute exercise session three times a week encourage healthy longevity.

Deep breathing. Life-giving deep breathing circulates throughout the brain and body, and works like an antioxidant, extending agelessness by purifying the blood, boosting cell renewal, defusing tension. Breathing influences the involuntary nervous system, which regulates the heart, circulation, digestion, and other vital functions. Breath control gets to the root cause of many ailments and restores balance. To have a deep inhalation, push more air out of your lungs when exhaling. Your lungs will then automatically take in more air. Over time, the length of an exhalation will equal the length of an inhalation. Usually, inhalations last longer.

Here are simple techniques to help you master proper breathing, a key to good health.

• To deep breathe, exhale through your mouth. Then inhale through your nose to a count of 4, starting with a slight inflation of the abdomen (place your hands on the abdomen and feel it come out then go in). Fill the lower lungs, then the upper lungs and expand the ribs. Hold breath for a count of 7. Exhale slowly through your mouth to a count of 8. This is one round. Notice when you inhale how the chest raises, shoulders go back and posture straightens. Do four rounds.

• You can do another excellent technique while walking or at home before an open window or door. Exhale through the mouth with a double aspiration one short, one long breath – that sounds like *huh-huhhh*. Immediately, inhale through your nose with a double inhalation – one short, one long breath. This is a complete breath. Do five to ten complete breaths daily. Think of filling your lungs and body with energy while your upper torso expands and straightens. Double breathing sucks more air into the lungs, focuses thought on breathing and relaxes.

• Try a one to two minute visualization. Close your eyes. See the light of the universe filling and healing your whole body (or a certain part) when inhaling. See all discord and limitation leaving your body when exhaling.

Follow by tensing the whole body from toes to head as you inhale – like a wave of energy – exhale. Tensing like deep breathing destresses mind and body. Tensing also tones muscles. It is hard to believe that doing something so simple can have such a profound effect, but it does.

*Do not hold the breath at any time
during planned physical activity and
especially during exercises. Let it flow.*

Posture. With good posture, the inner organs are in proper alignment and the lungs are not cramped. Through deep breathing, you get the feel of good posture. Your whole appearance is more positive. To anchor that feeling even more firmly in your mind, do the following often:

Stand with your heels three inches from a wall.
Let the wall support your head, shoulders, spine and buttocks.
Gently press the middle back to the wall. Don't strain! Notice how the tummy recedes as the navel moves toward the spine. The goal is to gradually feel the midback touch the wall.

Too often we are inclined to slump. Good posture needs to be remembered when we are sitting, standing and walking. Above all, be gentle with yourself. Don't force or criticize, be caring and careful. Small, steady steps eventually create giant leaps of progress.

Poor posture is the source of numerous physical problems. It contributes to illness and fatigue by restricting the breath and flow of blood to the vital organs, thereby interfering with digestion and elimination.

Note: The development of osteoporosis is not related to posture. It is a bone-thinning disease that can be prevented and treated with a calcium-rich diet, an exercise program that works the whole body, and, if needed, medication to prevent bone loss. Yogic exercises stimulate calcium retention in the bones by placing weight on the arms as well as the legs.

TEN EASY EXERCISES TO HELP YOU FIRM, TONE AND RELAX
You don't have to be an athlete to be in good shape.

The following warmups loosen the muscles and joints, increase flexibility and open channels for energy to flow. They work for the athlete and the couch potato. Many of these exercises are frequently incorporated in classes and mentioned in books and magazines. Some can be done while sitting. Wear loose, non-restricting clothing and no shoes.

Consult your doctor before beginning an exercise or sports program, especially when you have not had a physical activity routine.

Adopting at least 10-minutes of fitness activity into your daily routine three to five times a week doubles the body's depression-destroying hormone. How sweet it is when you feel more flexibility! *It's smarter and healthier to do five of these exercises rather than none.* Keep in mind the following:

The benefits.
Do them slowly. Patiently work your muscles without force or strain.
When one seems difficult, exhale as your body bends.
Deep breathe when holding a position.
Keep your mind in neutral.

The rush of adrenalin from working out energizes. It also puts the mind in positive gear. The more faithful you are, the more progress you will see, and the more benefits you will receive.

1. HEAD AND NECK ROLLS.
    Stand or sit erect, chin parallel to floor.
    – First, slowly move chin toward right shoulder, looking over your shoulder as far as possible, then move chin toward the left shoulder. Repeat 3 times.

– Second, drop chin to chest, slowly roll head to the left, lift chin slightly, then lower and back to chest. Do the same to the right and back to the chest. Repeat 3 times twice a day.
    Benefits: Relieves tension in head, neck, eyes, and shoulders. Stimulates circulation in the whole area including face and eyes.

2. SIDE BENDS.
    Stand or sit erect, chin parallel to floor and put hands on the waist.
    – Bend the torso as far as you can to the left keeping feet flat on the floor.
    – Then bend to the right. Do 3-5 times.
    Benefits: Stretching helps muscles work smoothly. This stretch works the side and torso muscles.

3. SHOULDER LIFT AND ROLL.
    Stand or sit erect. Lift shoulders to ears, hold briefly, then down to normal position. Do 3-5 times. Lift and roll forward and backward three times.
    Benefits: Feel the circulation. Relieves tension in the shoulder and neck area.

4. TORSO TWIST.
    Stand with feet 10-12 inches apart.
    – Raise arms up from the sides shoulder high and parallel to the floor, and straight.
    – Without moving the hips, swing arms to the left, bending the right elbow as you twist your body so the right hand touches the left shoulder and the left arm and hand is pointing at the wall behind. Keep feet flat on the floor and the eyes soft and unfocused.
    – Now repeat by swinging to the right. Do 3-5 times.

Benefits: Twists lateral muscles and torso like a corkscrew and contributes to slimming the torso when posture is erect. Relaxes eyes and body. Do 10 times before bedtime to unwind.

5. ARM CIRCLES AND EXERCISE FOR HANDS.
Small circles. Stand with arms at sides. Raise them shoulder high, straight up from your sides and parallel to the floor.
  – Clench fists and roll your arms in small circles, holding them straight, first in one direction 3-5 times, then in the reverse direction 3-5 times.
  – For extra stretch, turn palms up as you make the circles.

Big circles. Bring both arms up and around in big circles moving from the shoulders 3-5 times in one direction, 3-5 times in reverse.
Exercise for hands. Clench then unclench, straightening and stretching fingers and palms. Do 5 times.
  Benefits: Clenching and stretching the hands strengthens, energizes and assuages arthritis. The circles relieve tension, stimulate circulation in upper arms, wrists and hands, tone muscles, and help the heart.

6. RAISE HEELS AND LIFT ARMS FOR BALANCE AND POISE.
Check your posture before you begin, the straighter you stand the better your balance is.
  – Stand with arms relaxed at the sides and the feet hip width apart. Keep eyes glued to a spot on the opposite wall.
  – Inhale, exhale as you lift arms up over the head and raise your heels, putting your weight on the balls of your feet and toes. **When your balance wavers on your toes, stand with back**

braced against the wall as you raise arms and heels until your strength and balance improve.

- Inhale, exhale and lower your arms and heels with control until arms are relaxed at sides and feet are flat on the floor. Staying longer on the balls of your feet indicates stronger balance.
- Do 3-5 times.

> **Benefits:** Increases circulation, strengthens the feet and calves, improves balance, poise and coordination, giving a more graceful carriage. When you have good balance, you lower the possibility of falling and fractures by 25%.

7. WALKING AND RUNNING IN PLACE.

- Raise the <u>left foot</u> up so that the thigh is parallel to the floor. At the same time bend the right arm up at elbow and clench your fist as a **marching style**.
- Let your leg and arm go back down and relax your right fist.
- Raise <u>right foot</u> up so the right thigh is parallel the with floor. At the same time bend your <u>left arm</u> at the elbow and clench your left fist.
- Do 10 times, working up to 30 or more.
- When you can do 30 effortlessly, RUN IN PLACE or fast walk with arms relaxed and bent at elbows. Start with five to 10 times, work up to 30.

> Note: *By combining upper-and lower-body muscle activity, you expend more calories in less time and lose more weight than by exercising arms or legs alone.*

Alternative: Walk in place without raising knees and arms for three minutes. Then run in place for one minute. Tip: Try using double breathing.

> **Benefits:** Pumps your circulation, helps the heart and improves stamina and vigor. Brisk walking is one of the best, most underrated of all fitness

activities. When the weather is inclement, it's healthy to walk and/or run in place a couple times a day inside.

Don't hold your breath during exercising or sports. Exhale when it seems harder.

---

8. HEAD TO KNEES.

Sit on the floor with the tail bone, middle back and spine touching the wall.

 – Raise arms straight up over the head and stretch. Stretch legs out in front and press backs of knees to the floor.

 – Inhale and exhale as you slowly bend forward, stretching arms and hands to toes, bringing your head as close to the knees as you can and pressing backs of knees to floor. DO NOT STRAIN.

 – Relax, let head fall gently between arms. Breathe easily and count to 10.

 – Inhale and exhale as you raise torso with arms straight up over your head. Press back against the wall. Repeat 2-3 times slowly with control.

 Benefits: Massages the inner organs, stretches arm and leg muscles. Stimulates the spine, head and shoulders, increases flexibility.

9. LEG RAISES.

If you have back problems, check this one out with your doctor first. Lie on your back on the floor with your head on a pillow. This is easier if you bend knees and place both feet flat on the floor. Press the middle back to the floor several times. Then,

 – Bend one leg to your chest and squeeze gently.

- Exhale and lift this leg up, stretch straight and point toes to the ceiling, then your heel. Flex your foot like this several times. Lower your leg (or foot) slowly to the floor.
- Bend the other leg and bring the knee to your chest. Squeeze gently.
- Raise it up and stretch straight, point toes to ceiling, then heel. Flex the foot several times as you did with the other leg.
- Lower leg (or foot) slowly to the floor.
- Do two more times with each leg.

   Benefits: Stretches leg and ankle muscles, reverses circulation in legs; exercises mobility in hips; strengthens and conditions abdominal muscles.

10. BACK ROLLS WITH BENT KNEES.
   - Lie on floor with your head on a pillow and arms extended straight out from the shoulders.
   - Draw knees up to a center position in line with your torso.
   - With knees together and without moving shoulders or arms, exhale as you roll your <u>knees as far as you can to the right.</u> Simultaneously, <u>roll your head to the left</u>.
   - Hold for a count of 10. Feel the twist in your torso.
   - Exhale as you bring knees and head back to center. <u>Roll knees to the left side</u> and <u>your head to the right</u>. Hold for a count of 10, then back to center. The goal is to touch the sides of the bended legs to the floor without moving arms or shoulders.
   - Roll to each side three to five times.
   - With knees drawn up together in the center position, feel the lower back on the floor and place hands on knees. Roll your knees around several times as if they

were drawing an imaginary oval on the ceiling, first to the right, then to the left, massaging the lower back.
   Benefits: Relieves tension in torso and throat, stimulates circulation, increases midbody flexibility and stretches muscles in torso.

   FINALE. Stretch out on the floor. Tense all muscles in arms, legs, hands and throat. Release and take three deep breaths. Roll to your right side, bend knees and bring them up to your chest in the fetal position. This stretches your back. Close eyes and rest.

   Some of these exercises can be done outside where you can enjoy fresh air and sunshine. Doing several before bedtime relaxes the body and mind. When you see an exercise in a magazine or on TV that you like, add it to your list and create a menu of choices. Variety prevents boredom.

   Don't listen to the mind's babble of excuses for not doing what *you know* is good for you. When the babble begins, remind yourself of the benefits and *just do it*. Repetition is the key to mastery in everything. Choose today to make fitness a top priority because wellbeing follows. Be your own support system!

Give yourself time to "grow young."
Remembering to do these exercises and
the details of each, develops mental
clarity, memory, and the ability to reason –
important side effects.

   Caution! Overexercise can be harmful to joints and muscles. Dr. Kenneth Cooper, the heart physician who coined the word "aerobics" said overtraining can cause more harm than good. Women athletes have a higher injury rate than men in similar sports, especially knee injuries. Overdoing exercise results in stress that causes the body to take defensive measures. Seek a normal balance and use common sense.

SOME FITNESS OPPORTUNITIES

Build up fitness gradually. Moving from totally sedentary to moderately active is safe. Walking and moderate exercise produce good results with no bad side affects. Lack of exercise leaves you at greater risk for cancer, heart disease, and other ailments.

Listen to your body and exercise at your own pace. Fitness activity need not be strenuous to achieve benefits, but challenge yourself to gradually increase your vigor into some efforts. Vigorous exercise increases cardiorespiratory fitness. Take lessons from a qualified instructor when you want to learn a sport or exercise. Check out the local health and athletic clubs, senior and community centers for classes designed for 50-plus women.

Boost protein intake before and after exercise for stamina and muscle energy. Taking vitamin E before physical activity improves the body's response to exercise.

The Challenge. Sportswomen will tell you about the pains and joys of self-surpassing their abilities. When they silence the naysaying voices within and concentrate on the play, they discover new capacities. Winning is exhilarating and satisfying. But, we don't always win, so it makes good sense to learn detachment from the results of winning or losing. This detachment leads to equanimity. Granted, this is not easy. We need to constantly remind ourselves that the end goal for those of us who are not professionals is continuing mental and physical health, the fun of action, and camaraderie.

When we transcend the winner or loser mode and concentrate on execution, we find that sports and fitness endeavors refine our energies, focus our mind, release extraordinary capabilities, and fuel enthusiasm. By continuing in sports and/or any fitness program, we discover an interior freedom and grace far beyond our anticipated results.

> *The human body was designed*
> *and built for movement.*
> *Exercise works better than tranquilizers.*

Strength also called weight and resistance training. When we become stronger, we become more active. Loss of strength can be due to failure to use muscles as much as aging. *Regardless of your age,* you can achieve significant gains in muscle strength and bone density with weight training. It adds muscular support to joints by using an opposing force. The force can be free weights (dumbbells), elastic bands or machines specifically designed for this purpose. Do slowly for maximum benefits. The flexibility gained improves walking, climbing stairs, doing everyday chores, and sports. Studies show it is excellent therapy for arthritis. Instructors emphasize stretching and walking the track or in place are important before we do any fitness activity or sport in order to eliminate pulled muscles and soreness.

Golf. Patty Berg, who is over 80 and the first president of the Ladies Professional Golfers Association, said the greatest thing in the world is participation. Golf is a sport that most women can play for as long as they want to. One golfer said that at times it is as enjoyable as a root canal! But that can be said about almost anything. For better exercise, skip the electric cart and walk. Consult with a professional at a golf course about equipment and lessons. Senior centers also schedule lessons. As your muscle strength, stamina and technique improve, so will your game.

Tennis. Learn the game with an instructor. Develop strength and power in your torso, shoulders, arms and legs with weight training. This prevents pulling unused muscles and soreness. Making new friends and the sense of fun in action is worth the effort. One woman started classes in her 60s and became a top level player in two years, competing against women of all ages. Both doubles and singles are fun – you'll burn more calories with singles. The United States Tennis Association has a Seniors Breakfast League for doubles play. A 60+ woman who played in a PrimeTime tennis group biked two miles to the courts, played for one and one-half hours and biked home. She also bikes five miles to work when she's teaching. No sore muscles or lack of energy for that gal!

Bicycling. Increasing numbers of 50-plusers are biking around town and country. Seeing a community or the countryside on a bike is a treat. Bike tours are popular in the U.S. and Europe. Cities and states are continually developing wider biking paths according to the League of American Bicyclists in Washington, D.C. The League certifies instructors who teach classes on safety (helmets), maintenance and the art of cycling in many states such as Florida, Colorado, Arizona, Minnesota, California, Texas, Iowa, Washington and Oregon. Biking is good therapy and improves heart rate, strength and circulation.

Swimming and water exercises. Water is a safe effective exercise medium that is gentle yet demanding, conditioning as it tones. By cushioning joints, it eliminates stress and injury. At the same time, water affords 12 times more resistance than air. Water exercises and swimming are powerful aids to improving cardiovascular health, strength and agility without the impact of walking, running, skiing, or tennis. Water walking and aerobic exercise offer the same low-impact benefits as a good swim, reducing chronic muscle and joint pain while increasing endurance and balance. They also extend the range of motion after breast cancer surgery and restore lost functions to women with debilitating conditions. The Arthritis Foundation offers an aquatic program at health centers and YWCA. Call the national office at (800) 283-7800 or your local foundation chapter for more information. However, because water lessens the weight on the hips and spine, it does not appear to decrease the risk of osteoporosis as well as weight-bearing land exercises do.

One woman enjoyed aquacize classes at her senior center so much she began going to the pool five times a week and has made it a habit for years. Be sure an instructor is trained and certified in group aquatic exercise. You may want to observe a class in action. Take it easy at first and gradually increase your workout.

Walking. A brisk walk every day does a world of good with the least risk when compared to other exercises and at no cost. Walking improves digestion, reduces the risk of colon cancer and constipation. It burns calories, helps your respiro-cardio systems and can even lower blood pressure and prevent bone loss. You can do it anytime anywhere. Walk, don't drive, whenever you can.

Snow Skiing. Like most sports, skiing is twice as enjoy-able when you take lessons first. Cross country skiing rates very high for overall aerobic benefits. Flexibility is a must. Swishing through the sparkling snow with the warm sun on your face, up and down forested pathways and mountain slopes is a thrilling way to have winter fun. Cross country skiers pack their lunch so they can have it on the trail and feel the beauty of a mountain high. Women over 50 who down-hill and cross country ski have the glow of good health and good cheer.

Yoga. It can reverse the most obvious symptoms of aging! People who practice yoga daily show fewer signs of diseases and memory loss associated with aging. It stretches the "kinks" out of the body, improves posture, balance and coordination. Breathing is emphasized and benefited by opening up the chest. Yoga is one of the few exercise systems where weight is borne through the arms and upper body as well as the legs. Faithful participants retain flexibility well into their advanced years. Getting instruction from an experienced and learned teacher is best because learning the movements correctly can prevent improper positioning and too much strain on knee joints. The same can be said for t'ai chi.

For those who are recovering from surgery, in a wheelchair, overweight or are reluctant for any rea-son, upper body yoga exercises can help you. *Sitting Fit* is an audio tape by Susan Winter Ward, Certified

Yoga Teacher, created just for you. You, too, can do gentle, health-giving exercises while sitting that rejuvenate. To order this tape call toll free (800) 558-9642. Look for any exercises you can do sitting down, not just yoga.

T'ai Chi. In a serene, silent way, this martial art gives to body and mind most of the benefits of other exercises. Like yoga, it has been practiced since ancient times and is recognized as therapeutic and rehabilitative. A study at Baylor College of Medicine in Houston found that people who practice t'ai chi have better balance and feel calm, relaxed and centered. Its low-impact and emphasis on balance is also supported by the National Institute on Aging.

Women who dislike exercising and sports may enjoy classes in t'ai chi. At home, you can do a routine in five to ten minutes. No special equipment or sweating is required, just graceful slow motion. Awareness of posture, muscle movement and breathing from the diaphragm increase. T'ai chi is so gentle and effective that women in their 80s and 90s are taking classes. Regulars experience fewer falls. Yuk-Ying Ante, wife of Dr. Robert Ante, an Asian scholar and director of a t'ai chi institute, said it has given her a new attitude toward life. Now she is not afraid to grow old!

And that's not all! Women, 55 and older, are also competing on volleyball and softball teams and having lots of fun with tap, line and square dancing, even running. At one of the Bolder Boulder Races in Colorado, a little boy who was watching the racers from the sidelines yelled, "Hi, grama!" A few minutes later, his mom ran by and he yelled, "Hi, mom, grama's up there!"

Sports and exercise apparel. Invest in a good pair of shoes and socks suitable for the activity. When you find out how comfortable sports shoes are, you will want to wear them everywhere. A sports bra lessens bouncing breasts. Layered clothing is the way to go. As you get warmer, just peel it off. Bright colored sports apparel psychologically lifts your spirits and energy. Give everything that is old and dowdy to the needy. Don't use it for exercise classes! Treat yourself to cheerful-looking sports wear.

Water. Here we go again, but can we hear it too often? Drink before, during and after all exercise even aquatics – water that is, not caffienated coffee, tea or sodas. Warning signs of dehydration are fatigue, flushed skin, heat exhaustion, impatience, stumbling and dizziness. Water regulates body temperature and helps your body absorb the nutrients that give energy. Drink cold water on hot days and warm, on cold days. If you don't like water, put a dash of fruit juice in it or opt for a sports drink. Water controls overeating and is not retained as excess weight.

Hot weather safety tips. Wear a wide-brimmed hat or cap when in the sun. Avoid midday sun. Although sunscreens are oil-based and feel like moisturizers, they may lack the beneficial ingredients of a good moisturizing product. Moisturize first. Wait for it to be absorbed. Then, slather on the sunscreen at least 30 minutes before you go outside. Sunscreens are available for every skin type.

When it's hot outside, you can stabilize blood pressure, heart rate and body temperature during strenuous activity by wearing a tie saturated in cold water around your neck. An even better solution is the Kafka Kool Tie. This tie, designed in prints and solid colors, contains nontoxic polymer crystals. When soaked in water, they swell and stay cool. This simple precaution enables us to safely work, play and exercise without heat fatigue. Firemen have used it to stay cool in blazing heat. I wear it when playing tennis, golf and strength training during hot summer days. It helps. To get more information about this tie, call toll free (888) 566-5843.

Beat the heat!
Freeze water in a plastic bottle.

Stick with it like fly paper and remember the benefits! A woman may say, "Oh, I get plenty of exercise cleaning my house," or "I get in lots of walking at work. Who needs more exercise?" Housework and walking around the workplace burn few calories and do not relax or destress. In fact, most women carry their worries and anxieties along when doing both. With fitness activities or sports, our concentration on the execution relieves our thinking of other concerns and stirs the flow of adrenaline in a way seldom felt when doing housework or rushing from one office or file cabinet to another, not to mention the numerous physical benefits.

Design a fitness program with variety so that it isn't a drudge. For example, if you do t'ai chi or yoga, add to your plan brisk walking or a sport. A good routine gives you a happy high and you will be more likely to stick with it. Even if your weight stays the same, you are building muscle and using up body fat. Do not be too concerned with the pound number. In fact, forget it and keep up the activities that make you a healthier person. Diet partnered with planned physical fitness is required to maintain a desirable weight. It is THE way to prevent future weight gain and drive the joy of living.

Regularity, repetition and determination are the secrets of success. Fitness is the door to happy times and the realization that we can grow young. Reward yourself with a soak in a fragrant bath, Jacuzzi, sauna, a massage – some special treat or gift for you. This is an added incentive to sustain a plan for fitness *for a lifetime.*

A smile is the shortest distance between
two people. (Victor Borge)
And, your face needs the stretch!

CHAPTER 4

Look Like the
Vital Woman You Are!
Put Beauty in Your Picture

*"Let me grow lovely growing old
So many fine things do:
Laces, and ivory and gold,
And silks need not be new."*
– Karle Wilson Baker.

Why do people love cultivating gardens? Just because a garden is old, do we stop planting, pruning and watering? Why do we want our home to have pictures, decorative items, and comfortable furnishings? Just because our home is old, do we stop maintenance, painting, and renovating? You are 100 times more important than either home or garden. The appearance of a woman is no less a caring creation than is a garden or home. It takes a lot less time and leaves a lasting impression.

Intelligent women as far back as Cleopatra and Elizabeth I have known that their image had personal and social force. These women used bejeweled high fashion and cosmetics as a powerful tool and left a longstanding mark in history. In our times Margaret Thatcher always made an authoritative fashion statement as Prime Minister of Great Britain for 11 years. We will remember the grace, elegance and simplicity of Jacqueline Kennedy Onassis, one of the twentieth century's most unforgettable First Ladies. You have seen many 50-plus women on television who are stunning.

Appearance, more than anything else, affects the first impression we give. For better or for worse, it has always been influential. A businesswoman who had a double mastectomy said she didn't want people feeling sorry for her so she did everything possible to look her best wherever she went. It gave her personal comfort and confidence. Another woman who had the same surgery, worked part time in a hospital. She felt the same way and said she always smiled because it made her feel better, especially on sad days, and she noticed something amazing. Her smiling became like a mirror. Everyone smiled back. I mention these women because a mastectomy permanently depletes energy. It takes twice the effort to do anything.

"Don't you think it is shallow to be obsessed with appearance?" Yes, it is shallow to be obsessed by anything, and no one recommends it. But this is not about obsession. It is about attitude. Appearance reflects how we feel about our self *and our world*. It influences how we act and how people react to us. The purpose of color and style is to reveal the vitality and personality of the woman that is often dimmed by a drab exterior.

When I asked an audience why appearance was important, one women said, "If we don't care about ourselves first, how can we care about other people?" A Californian said to me, "I'm 75, feel 35 and that's the way I want to look." She was an active, enthusiastic woman who wanted her appearance to reflect that. It is not difficult to do and doesn't take lots of time or money. It's not vanity or egotism. When we have a winning image, we are happier. Our attitude is positive. Our outlook is upbeat. Our self-confidence soars.

"But, it's the inner beauty that counts most!" Many times, I have seen how applying lovely makeup colors to a face brings out beauty, the inner glow, that is not apparent from a "bare" face. This step in beauty care emphasizes the real woman who is hidden behind a bland, nondescript face. Becoming color makes the face ageless. It is not difficult; it does take desire and a caring touch.

Appearance talks to people about the person you are. Your outside persona reflects the inside person. An attractive total image is part of the formula for personal satisfaction and successful relationships. It shows the degree of respect for oneself and for people in general. We don't have to look like Whistler's Mother just because we have lived a few decades!

Divorced or widowed women may think, "What difference does it make how I look." Or, "I'm not dating any more, so why wear makeup?" The wife may think, "My husband doesn't care how I look and I'm not into all that glamour stuff. It's so vain anyway." The woman who doesn't think her husband cares can be assured he notices attractive women; why shouldn't she be one of them?

Every woman should take an honest look in the mirror to see if she is really content with her reflection. If she likes what she sees, she feels better about the woman she is. If she doesn't, helpful hints are in this chapter. An appealing appearance automatically attracts a positive response and friendship.

Remember the fascinating play, *Pygmalion,* and the musical, *My Fair Lady?* The main character is a bedraggled, beggarly woman who consents to be transformed into a charming beauty. We may not have the problems the woman in this story had but the years after midlife are a good time to consider transformation and renewal. Aging changes life patterns. We can degenerate or regenerate. Thousands of seniors are putting energy into regeneration. The are continuing education, exploring new adventures, starting businesses, learning new games and pastimes, pursuing new interests, improving their minds and bodies, and going for new horizons.

Adventure and opportunity are as available now as they were in our younger years. A life-giving attitude helps us to gradually abandon harmful habits and lifestyles and opens us up to new possibilities. The stereotypes of our mothers and grandmothers are gone forever. In this new era, we have more choices than they ever dreamed of. With hi-tech, speedy communication, burgeoning new ideas, and the helping hand spirit, we can refuse to be mesmerized by the age number and seek our personal dream even past midlife. Many women, before they reach the milestone of 50, have been occupied helping others and have had little time or energy to look after their own needs. This is the time to examine our thoughts, feelings and goals to see if they are creating the life we like.

"She's not my mother! She's my wife." Have you ever noticed couples and thought the man's wife was his mother? The man is tanned, well-groomed with tailored slacks and jacket and beside him is his wife with white hair, faded face, and yesteryear's clothing.

A woman who was in her late forties was married to an upward-moving young executive. Her hair was practically all white but she believed appearance was incidental. "People have to take me the way I am, white hair and all. Why should I change now? Besides, I don't care about all that fuss." In younger years it is easier to get by with that philosophy. After midlife, everything changes – how we think, look and act, and how we are perceived. If this woman clings to her "old" ideas, she may be seen as older than she actually is. Even worse, she may start to act like it!

There are always exceptions. The youthful-looking face with attractive makeup and white hair can be stunning. Another exception is former First Lady Barbara Bush. Even though her face was obviously older, her crown of soft white hair framing her face with lovely colorings was perfect.

One husband was so disgusted with his wife's hair that he made an appointment for her to have it colored and styled, took her to the salon and waited. When the work was done, she came out and said, "Hi, Harry." But he didn't recognize her! The change was astonishing and even better than he expected. He took her pridefully by the arm and escorted her out to a dinner date.

Although the following account is about men, some women may be guilty of the same thoughtlessness. A woman decided to put an ad in the "Companion Wanted" column of her local senior newspaper and lined up three coffee dates. The first man's breath was so foul it nearly knocked her off the chair. The aftershave cologne of the second man came around the corner before he did, and the third one wore bedroom slippers!

Daughters have called me and asked how they can encourage their mothers to look as good as they once did. It saddens them to see that their moms don't give a hoot about how they look. Maybe appearance is unimportant because of no romance, career, social life, etc. Do they realize a careless appearance can be depressing first to them, whether or not they admit it, and second, to their children and everyone they meet?

Often depression, a feeling that no one really cares, is the reason for a ho-hum appearance. Depression is like a scrawling weed and must be uprooted before it destroys the flowers of wellbeing. There is relief for this common malady. Healthy eating and staying fit generate the energy to get rid of sad thought and put more life into living.

The great comedian George Burns wrote in his book, *How to Live to Be 100 or More*, that the biggest danger of retiring [and the years after 50] is people start to rehearse being old. They start to take little steps, groaning, grunting and frowning. Their posture begins to slump and they start to look sloppy. He said the old saying "Life begins at 40" is silly. Life begins every morning we wake up. Modern thought advocates that good looks, good times, good eating and healthful activity are as much for us as for younger people. They are part of an effective self-care program.

Dr. Bernie S. Siegel in his book *Love, Medicine & Miracles* said that self-care is not selfish. It is a way to stay mentally and physically healthy. The image we manifest is part of self-care. Its cultivation gives us a renewed sense of life that cheers ourselves and our associates, relatives and friends. This involves using stylish simplicity, appropriate colors, and the many good products on today's market. A reader of my *Beauty Beyond 50* column wrote, "There are many of us over 55 who would love to look younger." To these women I say, do everything you can to look like the vital woman you are, and you will automatically look younger.

Be a distinctive asset in the workplace. Laws do not prevent a certain prejudice and ill will in society and the workplace against older people. We can lessen it by believing in ourselves, avoiding stagnation, and never stopping to learn and improve. Physical appearance does affect hiring decisions, especially if the job involves meeting the public. It may be wrong to judge by appearance, but it is a habit of the ages. The "dress for success scenario" is a truism. In the workplace it is desirable for us to have an energetic appearance as well as mind and attitude.

If you were running a business, you would want employees that inspired confidence in their customers or clients. Because of years of experience, the woman over 50 has a talent for this, especially when her looks are as sharp as her qualifications.

Which would impresses more interest and energy – a black and white photo of a flower garden, or one in color? For women who are still interested in working, serving or volunteering, attractive color on face and figure will give you the edge. Take the woman above who didn't give a hoot about her appearance – apply becoming color to her face, run a brush through her hair to fluff it up, remove the grey, black, navy or lackluster clothing, dress her in a pink, aqua or mint green suit and you have an attractive woman.

"But, I don't have the time!" Actually, it doesn't take a lot of time – at most, ten minutes to apply makeup for the day. To dress in simple styles with layering, allow five minutes. With a good haircut, you should be able to brush to separate, spray, pick to style and spray to set in five minutes. Every four to six weeks, save time and money and color your own hair. Allow 45 minutes to color and another 10 to set. Many spend more time than that in front of the television set!

HOW TO PUT BEAUTY IN YOUR PICTURE

The secret to looking like the vital woman you are is color. Color is logical because both the skin and hair lose pigmentation. When you know whether you look best in warm or cool colors, choice is easier. In makeup, this means blush and lipstick in blue-red, pinks, roses (cool) or orange-red, apricot and corals (warm). A color analysis to determine the colors that are best with your skin, eyes and hair saves time, money and worry in selecting makeup, clothing and even hair color.

Zap the wrinkles. Banish cigarettes! Nicotine causes veins to shrink, lines and wrinkles to flourish, and skin to become sallow, not to mention what it does to your lungs! To prevent squint lines wear sunglasses with UVA and UVB blockers. They are also an attractive accessory. Get enough sleep to provide time for cell regeneration as mentioned in Chapter 2.

Skin resurfacing with laser light, performed by a plastic surgeon or dermatologist, gives a smooth complexion without the pain and inconvenience of traditional facelifting treatments. Some women have said it is not as bad as going to the dentist. It has a risk factor of less than one percent without cutting, bleeding or chemicals. Consequently, the possibility of scarring or pigmentation problems is reduced. It removes spots, birthmarks, acne and chickenpox scars, precancerous lesions, unwanted blemishes, benign growths but not sagging. The results are a healthier, younger looking complexion.

Select a doctor who is skilled and experienced in skin resurfacing laser surgery. To find one in your area, call the American Society for Dermatologic Surgery (708) 330-9830. Because nothing prevents wrinkling or aging, the process can be repeated in five or ten years. After laser resurfacing, one very satisfied woman said, "No matter how old we get we still care about the face we present....It's an elevation [to my peace of mind] when I look the best I can."

Easy ways to keep your skin youthful. Switch from bar soap to a facial/beauty bar or liquid cleanser. For very dry skin, cleanse with almond or olive oil. It easily removes all makeup. To tighten skin blend in your palm one teaspoon each of honey and plain yogurt, smooth on your face and leave on for 10 minutes. Thoroughly rinse off. Egg whites do the same. Masking once or twice a week to deep clean and smooth the complexion makes foundation and all colorings look better, and it gives a glow to the dry complexion. Apply a moisturizer to damp skin, especially around the delicate eye area. A creme moisturizer has more emollients than a lotion.

Sunshine is beneficial. It is the fire of life and helps the healing process. Ten minutes exposure with little clothing and no sunblock is beneficial for your skin and bones, providing your skin is not sun sensitive. However, more than that can seriously damage and age the skin. Use a sunscreen with a sun protection factor of 15 when you expect to spend more than 10 minutes in the sun. Apply generously 20 minutes before you go outside. This protection also prevents more lines and wrinkles.

Alpha and Beta Hydroxy Acid Lotions and Cremes. Both of these exfoliators serve the same function. Beta hydroxy acids are gentler and better suited for skin that is sensitive to alpha hydroxy acids. BHAs may also be better for oily or combination skin types.

These hydroxy acid lotions and Renova, a retin A product which is obtained by prescription from a dermatologist, reverse the effects of sun damage and wrinkling, smooth skin texture and fine lines, even color, and lessen fine lines when used properly. They remove dead cells that do not come off with cleansing and give skin a satiny look, making it healthier.

Do not slather on AHAs and BHAs as you would a moisturizer. Use a pea size amount for the whole face. Applying too much or too often may cause flaking and redness. It takes about four weeks to shape up your skin if you have been neglecting it.

Managing rosacea. This facial condition is more common than people think. Rosacea, not booze, caused W. C. Field's ruddy, bulbous nose. At the present, there is no cure but women are successfully controlling the redness, flaking and blemishes. Pale complexions, especially those of Scottish,

Irish or Celtic descent, are more predisposed to rosacea. The following trigger flare-ups: a sunlight, heat on your face, excessive exercise, sweating, stress, alcoholic beverages, hot drinks, spicy foods and those that contain histamine such as tomatoes, spinach or chocolate.

Recommendations for skin care are: Metro Gel for oily skin and Metro Cream for dry, flaky skin (both available by prescription), plus a mild cleanser and moisturizer such as Cetaphil products (found in drugstores). Be meticulous about treating your complexion with a gentle touch and use only alcohol-and oil-free products. Ask your dermatologist about a beta hydroxy acid (BHA) creme to exfoliate and smooth your skin.

In the sun, wear a wide-brimmed hat and a non-greasy sunscreen with an SPF of 15 or 30. A green tinted concealant helps to cover the redness. Apply an oil-free foundation over the concealant for an even tone. Use non-greasy makeup, for example, a powder blush and Coty's lipstick, which has few emollients and stays on longer.

A dermatologist can prescribe a topical antibiotic for long-term therapy that incurs little risk. Severe ruddiness has been successfully treated by laser. For more information, write to The National Rosacea Society, 800 South Northwest Highway, Suite 200, Barrington, IL 60010. The toll-free number 1-888-662-5874. They publish a complimentary newsletter, Rosacea Review, that is available for the asking.

MAKEUP

The focal point of appearance is your face. It is far more interesting than clothing, so treat it with care! The lovely colorings of makeup beautify the whole image. On the faces of hundreds of women in my makeup classes, I have seen it "erase" at least five years. Blending and color selection are primary considerations. No neutral shades in lip color or blush for us! We need enriching color because the skin and hair both lose pigmentation. Minimal makeup is foundation, blush and lip color.

Don't rush it! When you hurriedly put a dab of color here and a dab there, that's exactly what it looks like. Put on only as much makeup as you have time to apply carefully. When you are farsighted, application is easier with a mirror that has triple or quintuple magnification. If you have never worn makeup, a beauty consultant or color analyst can help you in the privacy of your home or their studio. To find one, check out the classified pages in your phone book or ask your friends.

HOW TO ERASE YEARS FROM YOUR FACE

Foundation. Natural looking makeup starts with a good foundation that provides a finished base for blush, lip and eye colorings. Today's foundations are excellent and, with few exceptions, do not cause irritation. They protect as well as beautify. Many contain moisturizers and sunscreens. When the right shade in a good product is applied, it is undetectable and gives the complexion an even tone. Choose one that is formulated for "mature" skin with good coverage. "Sheer" coverage does little for the less than perfect face. Select an enriching shade, not so dark that it looks like a deep tan, nor so light that your face is pale and pasty. Too light a shade is a common mistake. Apply with a gentle, downward stroke (upward is for cleansing and moisturizing). Smooth over the whole face, eyelids if you wish, and around the jawbone but not on the throat.

Eye makeup. A thin brow line ages faces that have lines and wrinkles. It is easy to correct. Draw them thicker with a brow pencil or powder. Blond is a good shade for white, grey and blond hair. Thicken and darken lashes with mascara. Extra lashes are easy to apply and de-age the eyes. You can even get blond ones. They do make a difference! Keep eye shadow whisper soft in pastels and earth tones. Eye lining defines eyes when lashes are sparse or light.

Blush. It gives your face a healthy hue and brings out the color of your eyes. Make it a blend, a shimmer of color, not a spot. Blend it on the cheekbone areas, not on the smile lines.

Lip color. Light up the whole face with lipstick. Line lips with a lip pencil to give a clear outline, improve the shape and make lips fuller. Brighter shades detract from the double chin.

Makeovers. Wherever free makeovers are offered, trot on down and get one! You will always learn something and they help you to stay up-to-date. You will not be influenced to buy the wrong colors if you know whether you have warm (yellow) or cool (pink/blue) skin tones. A color analysis makes shopping easier.

FASHION FACTS FOR SAVVY WOMEN

• Be aware of how your body shifts and changes over time and adapt your style. What looked good last year may not work this year.

• Don't dress according to your age! Being 50, 60, 70, or more doesn't mean we dress older. We may not want to wear thigh-high skirts, reveal too much skin, or wear figure-revealing clothing. But that leaves lots of room for panache, elegance, casual, and fun-to-wear apparel. Forget the age number and let what you wear say who you are.

- Beauty comes in all sizes and shapes. Your size does not determine your beauty potential. Self-thought does. The fashion industry designs for size 16 and over. Dresses with large bold colorful prints give a striking look to the big woman, as do slimming one-color suits.

- Simplicity in style, vitalizing color, and one-or two-color outfits accented with a neutral color (i.e. white, gray, beige, brown, navy, black) creates a smart look. Stay away from drab colors and go for cheerful ones, a rainbow of happy shades. The colors around the throat reflect up to the face. Be sure to wear you most becoming shades here.

- Black does not flatter the face that has lines and wrinkles. It is better worn below the waist, never around the face unless the neckline is cut deep and a wide border of skin frames the face. If you love black, be sure to have rich tones in your makeup because black as well as white drains color from the face.

- Flowing fabrics are more flattering than clinging textures that outline every bulge and make us look fatter.

- Wear higher hems when you are 5'3" or under and when your legs are slender and pretty.

- Body-hugging shoulder pads square the torso, "narrow" the waist and hips, and keep the lines of your garments crisp.

- Choose a bra with wider straps that do not put pressure on your shoulders. Thin straps can dig in and over time cause various aches and pains in the head and shoulders and even nerve damage to the neck. A good bra makes your clothes hang better and eliminates the matronly profile.

• For the full-figured woman, keep pins, brooches and scarves around the shoulders, not the bust.

• Women are wearing sport shoes and sneakers where they used to wear pumps. Businesswomen hurry around Manhattan in smart tailored suits and Reeboks. The Hollywood fashion setters (over 50 gals) wear sneaks with silk pant suits, red ones to match a red suit or color coordinated white down to white tennis shoes. How much better than torturing the feet in spiked heels! Exercise 6 on page 51 strengthens the feet. For dressier occasions, fashion-wise shoes with heels under two inches are found in different colors and skins.

Where is your hair headed? On bad hair days, put on makeup first. Color on your face interacts with the color in your hair to make it look better. Here's a quick hair fix: First brush or finger comb your hair to fluff. Spray with hair spray to give body and shine. Then use a hair pick to separate and shape to the style you want. Check the back with a mirror and pick into shape where needed. Spray again to set.

Wear the hair length you like whether it's short or to the shoulders. The length is determined by facial contours, body shape and lifestyle. Some women do not like short cuts and do not look good in one. A good hairstylist will never advise every woman over 50 to have a kinky perm and short hair. One boilerplate style for all of us went out with housedresses. The best style for the active woman is one that is soft and flowing. However, the tight, short perm is useful for women who are ill or cannot take care of their hair.

Coloring your hair raises morale because it de-ages the face. More and more women are coloring, and not perming, their hair. They find their hair has more shine, less breakage, and is healthier by eliminating one chemical process. Coloring thickens the shaft, as perming does, and makes hair more manageable.

A more natural looking curl is created by using Velcro curlers or the steam roller curling system. The latter takes about 15 minutes to set and is less drying than electric curlers. They are found in drugstores and beauty supply stores. Be sure to get small rollers if your hair is short. Women with straight-as-a-pin hair successfully use either of these methods. They save money, time and get a softer, more natural curl. Flowing and wavy is more youthful than tight and kinky. A curling iron helps in a pinch.

One woman told me that when her daughter's friends thought she was a grandmother, she knew it was time to get rid of the grey. An athletic woman, 68, was unhappy because her snow white hair made her look older than she felt. She had it colored a soft blond. At a family reunion, many said she seemed to be the only one who wasn't getting older! Grey or white hair is more attractive on women with cool skin tones than those with warm skin tones. This woman had warm skin tones – another reason why she didn't feel comfortable with the white.

Dark brown and black hair emphasize lines and wrinkles. Ash (cool) and golden (warm) blond and red are becoming hair colors at any age.

Help your hands. Nails snap with color excitement and give hands more grace when they are polished with a luscious color. Nails grow longer when lacquered. If you have problems, such as splits, breakage or ridges, women have found it helpful to coat with Nailtiques, a nail protein treatment. Nails are made of protein and love it. Nailtiques can be used alone and as a base under polish. It is found in beauty salons or call (800) 272-0054 or (305)378-0740.

Tanning lotions and sprays. A fake tan can look like the real thing. It is a safe way to get the sunkissed, healthy-looking glow. A couple of applications will give you the tone you want. It is a bonus when you start outdoor sports, go on a cruise, or just want the tanned look for warmer weather. Use it on the face and backs of your hands to diminish age spots and cover imperfections on your arms and legs. Go lightly on lines, wrinkles, elbows, knees and ankles which may tan darker. Be aware that your skin will burn unless the tanning product has sunscreen protection.

The directions explain how to apply, how long for drying and reapplication. Exfoliate first because the smoother the skin the more even the tan. Use a loofa or dry brush on the body and mask/exfoliate the face to get rid of rough areas. Then bathe. While skin is warm and moist, apply the tanning lotion in a circular motion. Wash hands immediately or they will be stained.

Bad breath is a big bugaboo. Ninety percent of all bad breaths are sulphur gases produced by an over abundance of bacteria on the tongue. The ridges on the tongue and the tongue's microscopic hairs harbor foul-smelling bacteria. The solution is ancient: Brush the tongue. Its advantages have been known for centuries. Today's periodontists recommend it for healthier teeth and gums. For us folks over 50 whose gums may be receding, tongue bacteria can result in root decay. Use a soft-bristled brush and stroke outwards from the rear of the throat as far back as you can without gagging. Put a mouthwash on your brush if you like. Drinking more water disperses the bacteria in your mouth.

Dr. Steven M. Wieder, D.M.D. of Sarasota, Florida has spent years researching halitosis. He developed a Tung-Brush™ and Tung-Gel™. The shorter, firm bristles of the Tung-Brush penetrate and cleanse the ridges quickly. Some dentists supply them or you can call 1-800-692-4949.

Until your breath is sweet-smelling, you may wish to tongue-brush two to three times a day. Nowadays, we are keeping our teeth for a lifetime and brushing the tongue is good insurance. For you romantics, you will be even more kissable!

A hint to pamper yourself and save time. A bath is more than cleansing. When you step into a bathtub, have tools for self-care within reach. While you relax in the warm scented water with soft music and maybe a candle or two burning, have at hand dental floss, a mask for your face, and orange stick to push back your cuticles. The mask will give your face a deep cleansing, flossing your teeth is good for teeth and gums, and pushing back soaked cuticles with an orange stick is healthier for the nail bed than prodding dry cuticles with a metal tool.

Stand tall! Good posture protects back muscles and slims your silhouette. When we slump the tummy protrudes. Holding the torso as erect as possible while sitting, walking and exercising is health-giving – the inner organs, heart and lungs have space to function and are not cramped. If you cannot hold an erect posture, you may need to strengthen your body with exercise or weight training. Weight-training increases muscle strength.

To get the feeling of good posture, stand against a wall, heels four inches away and with the shoulder blades, waist, tail bone, and buttocks touching the wall. Feel the shoulders go up and back, the chest expand and stomach flatten. This pose tilts the pelvis and is the stance you want to simulate.

Another way you can check your posture is: Take a deep inhalation, let the breath push the abdomen out slightly, expand the lungs and rib cage. The shoulders automatically go up and back and the tummy goes in. Exhale.

Two exercises for upper back squeeze that help posture:

Stand, bend elbows, palms down. With shoulders relaxed, inhale and exhale as you pull your elbows back, drawing shoulder blades together. Hold and count to ten. Slowly move elbows back to start position. Repeat several times.

Stand and interlace fingers behind your back over your buttocks. Inhale and exhale as you straighten arms and lift them as high as you can without strain. Feel your chest open and shoulder blades move. Hold and count to ten. Repeat a couple times. (Consult your doctor before beginning any exercise.)

Good posture gives you an alert persona and helps you to look like the vital woman you are. The tummy flattens, and clothing looks better.

You are unique! Let go of unrealistic expectations and stop comparing yourself with others. Be the "you" you want to be. Caring about our self prevents problems and is not egotistical. Often we are the only one who cares! Self-care blossoms into contentment and increases the joy of being with people. Don't get stuck in an image that dates you. Periodically reassess the style and color of your hair, makeup and dress. Strive for simplicity. Stick to a basic style that feels good. At the same time, be refreshed and try trendy new stuff. Sometimes it is as welcome as a spring breeze! Wear flattering colors whether they're "in" or not. Break bad beauty habits forever – no more sunbathing, smoking, fads, or neglecting what's good for you.

Think beautiful thoughts (about yourself, too!) – loving, caring, unselfish, patient, respectful, gracious, considerate, understanding, supportive, helpful, tolerant. They generate beauty.

Summary: How to keep age out of image!

Stay up-to-date. Use good products to maintain radiant skin, hair and body. Allow time for nurturing and beautifying, mentally and physically. This is value time.

Eat healthy and you will be happier. The USDA recommended allowances of Vitamins E, C and beta-carotene have mega benefits for your skin and hair. Drinking water hydrates the whole body including the skin – very important.

Exercise "oils" the joints, it also shapes up your figure, adds sparkle to your eyes. The increased circulation makes your skin and hair glow.

Wake up the faded, old look. Wear rainbow pastels, electric brights, earthy tones, nothing dull or drab. The vibrations of lighter colors are more positive than dark shades. Enhance your face with enriching colors. They will lift your spirits and lessen imperfections. Coloring hair is a morale booster, or, whiten the white and silver the grey.

Remember good posture. When you stand, sit, walk and exercise – head straight, shoulders relaxed and down. Tuck your pelvis under and don't arch your lower back.

Be involved to stay upbeat. You will have an added incentive to look and feel nifty. Sharing joy, helping when needed, working and playing as a team bring joy into your life.

Enjoy the outdoors. Sunshine on your face and body and the magnificence of nature are healing.

Smile! A sage friend said the first muscles to go are the little ones that hold up the corners of the mouth. Dale Carnegie wrote a chapter on smiling in his timeless book *How to Win Friends and Influence People*. This simple act – with sincerity – brightens your day and that of a lonely person. The best "you" shines through and you will be more attractive. Great thinkers recommend it.

Read something inspiring every day. Lighten up and look for laughs. He who laughs, lasts. Catch sad, critical thoughts and throw them out before they score a home run. Pursue a spiritual quest to give solace to your soul, rest to your heart and peace to your spirit.

Practice growing young, not getting older! A spiffy appearance is part of the formula. It best expresses the vibrant you. Do whatever beauty work is necessary, then forget it, and enjoy the flow of life.

Did you hear that? Someone whistled at me!

CHAPTER 5

The Best of Beauty Beyond 50 the Nationally Syndicated Column by Jo Peddicord

Today's woman over 50 is not waiting for life to roll by. She is grabbing and squeezing it for all it's worth.

The following excerpts contain more top tips to help you look nifty after fifty.

SKIN CARE

Q: *My face is very, very dry. What can I do about it?*

A : One cause is dehydration, which can be serious. Correct by drinking more water. Oranges and orange juice also benefit the skin. Ingest some kind of oil daily. By drinking a cod liver oil cocktail described on page 35, you lubricate skin, hair, the body linings and help arthritis.

Use alcohol- and fragrance-free products labeled "for dry skin." Soap is drying. Use a bar without "soap" in the name, such as a beauty bar, or a cleansing cream or lotion. Rinse thoroughly – 5-10 splashings. Moisturize when skin is damp to get the best absorption. Cetaphil Moisturizing Cream is an excellent remedy. When your hands have to be in water, add vinegar to counteract dryness.

Masking or applying an alpha hydroxy acid lotion gives a healthy glow to your face. AHAs do a good job of refining lines and improving texture – the higher the percentage of AHA in a product, the quicker it works. Some even fade age spots. Do not slather on! Apply a small amount for the whole face and throat once a day. Applying too much too often will sensitize the skin.

Steaming also moisturizes, deep cleans, tones, and plumps up lines. Facial steamers are found in beauty supply and drugstores. Steaming once a week before masking doubles the benefits.

Q: *You mentioned exfoliating in a column. What does that mean, and how can a woman with dry skin that looks like an alligator's wear foundation?*

A : Exfoliating and masking produce the same results. They remove dulling, dead cells that impede moisturizing and are not removed by cleansing. The accumulation of this surface sludge creates a dull, flaky, bumpy complexion. Remove them and skin is smoother and healthier. The resulting texture provides a better surface for foundation. Most cosmetic companies have masks and exfoliators. Apply to a cleansed face, leave on for ten minutes, rinse off. Then, moisturize.

When I emphasized the importance of masking during a makeup class, one middle-aged woman blurted out, "I have tried it many times and my skin always breaks out!" I said it is still a good idea but do not mask over skin eruptions. Six weeks later she phoned to say she started masking again, following my advice. The breakout stopped; now her face looks better than it has for years, she said.

Q : *In a column, you mentioned alpha hydroxy acids as alternatives to retin A. Can you tell me more about them?*

A : These organic acids, derived from plant foods and identified as light skin peels, are useful. Daily application over a period of time fades discolorations, softens lines and smooths the skin by mild peeling. This rejuvenating process creates radiant and youthful skin. Just apply a small amount to the whole face. Lactic (sour milk) and glycolic (sugar cane) acids are the most common. Some have moisturizers. Prices range from $7 to $50.

Q : *Do moisturizers really work? Do I have to pay a lot of money for a good one?*

A : A good moisturizer is especially important when skin is exposed to forced air heat, air conditioning, and cool weather. Cetaphil, Moisturel, and Complex 15 are dermatologist-recommended. They have no greasy after-feel and heal severely dry skin. A creme has more emollients than a lotion.

Q : *Are the infomercials and beauty products we see on television reliable and worth their price?*

A : Some products, such as Neutrogena and Alpha Hydrox, are reliable and not overpriced. Sophisticated packaging and advertising add to the cost, as you know. Drug and grocery stores have good products at affordable prices.

SURGERY

Q: *Many of us are interested in facelifts since they have become more common. Would you comment on this?*

A: Be wary of exaggerated and sensational claims in the media. To get the facts, a representative member of the plastic surgery community in Denver, Colorado said it's vitally important to consult with a *board certified, experienced plastic surgeon.* Names are available from the American Society of Plastic and Reconstructive Surgeons in Chicago. The toll-free number is 1-800-635-0635. Ask for those in your area who specialize in facelifts.

The condition of the skin and overall mental and physical health determines whether a woman is a good candidate for this surgery. Do it only for yourself...for your own comfort, self-esteem, maybe career enhancement, for no one else. Because smoking decreases blood circulating to the skin, some surgeons will not consider a smoker, others, only if she quits smoking a couple of weeks before the operation. Risk is always a factor in any surgical procedure. During the initial patient/doctor consultation, a woman should ask for referrals from his clients. This increases her understanding of the doctor and she gets a layman's thoughts about the procedure and results.

One woman in her mid-50s feels wonderful about her new face and throat. She got rid of the things that disturbed her – a wrinkly neck and sagging jowls. Although it took her six months before she felt fully recovered, her friend who is sixtyish underwent the same operation and returned to work two weeks after surgery. Both women are conscientious about complexion care and makeup. A couple of cosmetic surgeons said that women reap full returns on their investment when they learn to use makeup.

Less complicated solutions are collagen injections and laser skin resurfacing. The latter has a one percent risk factor. It involves no cutting, bleeding or changes in pigmentation. Results are impressive. It does not work for heavy wrinkling. Collagen injections are easy procedures that plump up lines. Both are done in the doctor's office. When signs of aging disturb you, these alternatives are valid considerations and healthier than withdrawing into depression.

Q: *I'm 5'4" and weigh 150 pounds and most of that has settled in my stomach. I'm overeating, I know, and would like to start looking my best again. Are tummy tucks safe?*

A: Yes, they are safe IF YOU GET A REPUTABLE SURGEON. This is no place to scrimp on money. It is worth the expense to have good work. A woman who is a cosmetic tattooist and works with plastic surgeons had this done and she looks slim and trim. She knew competent surgeons and chose one of the best.

A consultation is free. Talk to one or two highly recommended surgeons, and pick one you feel comfortable with. After you talk to them, you will have a good idea about what is involved and if you want to do it. Beforehand, list your questions, such as: How safe is this operation? What are the potential side effects and how long will they last? How many of your patients have needed additional surgery? May I contact former patients who have had this surgical procedure? How much will it cost? My book *Look Like A Winner After 50* discusses selecting a surgeon.

Whether or not you have surgery, a healthy diet AND EXERCISE are necessary to have a normal weight and good health. Both take off the pounds, but you can't just do the diet without exercise when you are serious about controlling your weight and looking your best. Any kind of regular exercise never fails to make a woman feel better. When the goal is to lose pounds, it doesn't necessarily matter how long (30 minutes is best) but that you do it every day.

Women who exercise at least four times a week seldom overeat. This is a lifelong program. Doing it for a few months or a year will not have long lasting benefits. It may be an uphill battle but it is one that leads to a good self-image, personal satisfaction and an active body, mind and lifestyle. Feeling good about oneself is a rewarding victory.

AGE SPOTS

Q: *I have fair skin and brown age spots on my face, arms and hands. How can I fade them without damage to my skin?*

A : New ways to do this are continually being developed. The safest way is to consult a dermatologist who can advise the best solution for your skin. Ask a dermatologist about liquid nitrogen. This is an inexpensive procedure that fades the spots in 10 days to two weeks. Retin A is costlier, takes about six months and yields beautiful results. At first, skin should be monitored by your doctor. A qualified physician who is experienced and certified in skin resurfacing laser surgery can remove them with a laser beam. Healing takes from seven days to two weeks.

The most inexpensive solution is a mixture of Porcelana Hydroquinone 2% and an alpha hydroxy acid lotion with a concentration between 6% and 12%. (Some AHAs have the percentage printed on the package.) You can find both products in drugstores. Mix a little of each and apply. It may take about six months to fade the spots. To be safe, try a little of the mixture on a small area and see how your skin reacts. Because sun exposure darkens the spots and interferes with any treatment, use an SPF 15 sunscreen.

Cosmetics help, too. Apply a concealant to facial spots, dust with powder to make it last longer, and smooth over with a foundation that covers well. A spray-on tanning lotion makes them less noticeable on your hands and arms.

MAKEUP

The skill of makeup application is a special bonus to all women over 50 when skin starts to fade. Once learned, they will see in the mirror a reflection that is five to ten years younger. Not only that, but the color of makeup brings out our vitality. The bland-looking face in no way defines us. Even a little makeup takes age out of image.

Q : *I've been told we should wear less makeup as we get older, but I think we need more. Who is right?*

A : You are. Because the skin and hair lose color as we get older, the face is renewed and our hair looks surprisingly better when we add the lovely colors of makeup. It is indispensable to erasing the faded look we may have. For example, foundation covers imperfections and discolorations, giving a porcelain finish; eye makeup defines eyes that hide behind glasses and blush brings out their colors; lipstick cheers up the whole face. Application doesn't take tons of time or buckets of bucks and is worth every cent and second it takes. Women feel more positive when they look in the mirror and are pleased with their face.

Q : *How should I wear makeup so that I don't look "made up?"*

A : The secrets of natural-looking makeup are: cleansing and exfoliating, a foundation, the right shades, careful blending, and, don't overdo. Exfoliation with an alpha or beta hydroxy lotion makes the complexion smoother. Moisturizing softens lines.

The total effect should be beautifying. No color should stand out and grab attention, such as sky blue shadow or heavy black eye lining. Coverage is important for foundation and blending is important for everything. By wearing all-cool or all-warm shades, depending upon the undertones of your skin, we create the harmony of color that complements the whole face and not just one feature.

If you have lots of lines, opt for a matte foundation. Wear blush, either rose, mauve, blue-red (the cool shades), or peach, coral, orange-red (the warm shades). Blend it along the cheekbones and toward the middle of the ears. No dabs of color and keep it off the smile lines.

Lipstick matches blush and lights up the whole face. With a lip lining pencil, outline the perfect shape – slightly outside the border to make thin lips fuller – then fill in with lipstick. The fewer the emollients, the better it will stay one. Coty's has a good one.

Eye shadow, eye liner and mascara bring out nondescript eyes. Use earth tones for eye shadow. Apply it darker along the upper lash line and diminish color up toward brows. Either a pencil or pen eye definer gives the eyes more emphasis especially when you have few lashes. Add color to brows with an eye brow pencil. Color lashes with mascara – black is the most popular color.

Always check your finished look in daylight, the best light, and touch up where needed. Applying makeup is fun because of the amazing results. It energizes your appearance and increases self-confidence.

Q: *I see so many women with blobs of rouge, blue shadow on wrinkled eye lids, and big red lips. Yet, you say we should wear makeup. I'll take my plain, lined face any time.*

A: You are talking about faces with the wrong colors applied incorrectly. Hundreds of women ranging in age from 20 to 90 have attended my makeup classes. They come to class wearing no makeup and leave smiling because they see how makeup turns their embarrassingly plain faces into attractive ones. This new face gives more self-confidence and makes them feel better about themselves. I have never seen a lined, colorless face that did not look 100 percent better and more youthful with correctly applied makeup. Plain is fine for the recluse but not for active women in the 1990s. Makeup is not hard to apply. It does take extra effort and time, but the transformation compensates for this. I do not favor makeup coloring that draws attention to it rather than the person. The purpose of makeup is to emphasize the beauty of the woman, not the makeup.

Q: *I have never worn foundation. With this pale face, I think it might help. Where do I start and will it do any good?*

A: Nothing beats a quality foundation to give the face a healthy tone. Its role has been underrated. Many women are averse to using it because it "feels heavy" or causes breakout. Today's foundations are lightweight and, with few exceptions, do not cause irritation. Many contain moisturizers and sun-screens. Plastic surgeons recommend makeup including foun-dation to women who have had facelifts. They know the value of expensive facelifts and other corrections is fully realized with the enhancement of makeup.

The natural look that most women want starts with a good foundation. Get one that gives good coverage. Sheer coverage or too pale a shade does nothing for the less than perfect face. When the right shade in a good product is applied, it is undetectable and gives the face an even patina. Department stores have a larger selection of shades. Test either on your face (if makeup-free) or on the back of your hand or inside wrist. See how it reacts with your skin. Often a slightly darker shade give the face a more attractive tone.

Apply with a gentle, *downward* stroke (upward is for cleansing and moisturizing). This enables it to cover better. Smooth over the whole face, eyelids if you wish, and around the jawbone, not on the throat. Foundation creates the fin-ished base for blush, lip and eye colorings. The natural look is almost impossible without it. Compare a plain face to one with becoming makeup and you will instantly see the impact of colorless vs. color. The flatter power of makeup beautifies our whole image.

Q : *My hair and skin are white and the foundation I use matches my throat like it's supposed to, but I look like a ghost with all the whiteness. Can I do anything about this?*

A : Nature lightens skin as well as hair. Wear a richer shade of foundation and you will have a better contrast between your complexion and hair. Pale skin needs a deeper shade of foundation so the skin has more vitality. Why not color your hair?

Q: *I'm a young 69 and always like to look my best. What do you think of women like me wearing eye makeup?*

A : Many celebrities who are over 50 wear it beautifully and so can you. I'm for anything that makes us feel good about ourselves. It is always appropriate for us to have a touch of glamour. Properly applied, it draws attention away from lines and wrinkles. Wear it because: It defines the eyes when lashes become few, grey or short. It lightens dark or veiny lids. It makes brows more youthful. Eyes are more expressive with it than without it.

Q: *Now that my hair is grey and there are more lines around my eyes, is it still okay to wear black eye liner as I always have?*

A : Adapting makeup to the changes in hair and face keeps us up-to-date. The way we have been wearing makeup for the last 20 years may not be appropriate now. Heavy black eye lining on fair-skinned women who are over 50 is too dark. If you prefer black, keep the line narrow. Why not try a newer shade such as grey, taupe, or sage green? Whenever any eye, cheek or lip color is overpowering, attention is drawn to it rather than the woman.

Q : *When I put on mascara it either blobs or flakes below my lashes. What is wrong, the product or me?*

A : Return all cosmetics that don't work as advertised. Stores send them back to the manufacturers and do not lose. Manufacturers should know when their products are unsatisfactory. Let's assume the product is a good one.

Try this. Apply mascara to upper and lower lashes. Blot with a tissue to remove excess, being careful not to press lashes against the skin. If you do, remove mascara that is on your skin with a cosmetic tip. Separate lashes with a lash comb or an old, clean mascara wand.

Q : *I plucked my brows decades ago and now they are really scarce. What can I do to make them look better?*

A : Use a blond, taupe or light brown brow pencil or powder, black if your hair is black, to make them fuller. Draw the brows over the inner eye corners one-fourth to one-half inch thick, the way they looked when you were younger. Draw the color across your brow bone and fatten your brows with short strokes, tapering to outer points – the way they grew originally. Do this slowly and carefully. When you use a brow pencil, finish by blending with a small brush. Fuller brows are better looking and more youthful than the severity of skinny ones.

HAIR

From the standpoint of personal confidence, finding a good hairstylist and cutter is almost as important as finding a good doctor. Attractive hair starts with a good haircut.

Q: *I heard a New York hairstylist say on TV that all older women should wear their hair short. I don't like short hair. Is he right?*

A: No, he isn't! Although many women over 50 look better with short hair, some will never wear it. The longer length is more flattering to the contours of their face and figure, and they are more comfortable with it. One length of haircut can't possibly flatter everyone. We are all uniquely different. If a woman has a slender, long throat, the longer length is better. If she has a short throat, the shorter length is better. The length works in harmoney with the contours of her head and figure.

Hairdressers frequently recommend the shorter cut because hair that is two or three inches below the ears tends to "draw" facial lines down. However, this can be corrected with makeup.

I saw the mother of a well-known actor on TV. She was in her 70s and had a soft flowing shoulder length hairstyle, full and waving. Her makeup was perfect. Even with noticeable facial lines, the lovely hairstyle and flawless makeup made her beautiful and a joy to watch. Incidentally, she had a sparkling personality, which didn't hurt either.

Q: *What hairstyle looks best with a round face?*

A: High on top and close to the head at the sides, with wispy curls framing the face. Tight curls and completely straight hair accentuate lines. To style, spray with hair spray; use a hair pick to raise the hair on top for height, spray again to set. Blended makeup colors on the face make hair look better. This is not pie in the sky. I see it all the time in my makeup classes.

Q : *How should I wear my hair? It is baby fine, thinning and starting to grey on the sides. My face is narrow with a high forehead.*

A : Products that add body and the texturizing cut will give you the look you want. If the greying bothers you, color it. Coloring or a body perm swells the shaft, making hair fuller and easier to manage. Balance your facial proportions with fullness on the sides and not high on top. Height emphasizes the length of your face and you want to balance it with fullness on the sides. It can be swept back or forward, or just soft curls but keep the hair on the sides full. A good hairdresser knows the texturizing cut that adds fullness to thin hair. Too short may be too severe. Let wispy, not kinky, curls border the forehead.

Q : *What do you suggest for hair that is very fine and limp?*

A : The reconstructive solution is a shampoo and conditioner specifically labeled for fine hair. Body-building products are designed to strenghthen the shaft and usually contain collagen (protein), panthenol, magnesium and biotin. Avoid products with petroleum jelly or lanolin. The molecules in these ingredients are too large to enter the shaft and benefit the hair. Permanent coloring and/or a fine-hair body wave adds volume by creating a fatter shaft. The result is thicker hair. Hair spray specifically for fine hair adds volume.

Q : *My hair has been over-permed and lost all of its shine. What can I do to remedy this?*

A : Don't get perms for a while and then only a body perm when absolutely necessary. Expose your hair to as few chemicals as possible. Even when hair is normal, try to make do with two or at the most three perms a year. Until your hair normalizes, maintain your own curl, starting with a good haircut. You can use velcro curlers or a steam roller curling system. The latter takes about 15 minutes to set and curl and is less drying than electric curlers. They are found in drugstores and beauty supply stores. A curling iron helps in a pinch. Women with straight-as-a-pin hair successfully use either of these methods. They save money and time and create a softer, more natural-looking curl. Flowing and wavy is more youthful than tight and kinky.

Use a shampoo and conditioner specifically for chemically treated or damaged hair. Since hair consists of protein and thrives on it, you want protein-rich products. Or, consult with an experienced hairdresser who can recommend treatment and products. Salons have excellent choices. A hair spray that adds shine will give you highlights. Diet and exercise also contribute to healthy shiny hair.

Q : *My salt and pepper hair gets a yellowish tinge along the forehead. I don't want to make it to Hollywood but can you give me a lift with this problem?*

A : This is a common problem with grey or white hair. A couple causes for yellowing are minerals in the water or smoke. You want your hair either silver grey or snow white, not a muddy shade in between. Even if you do not smoke, exposure to it can cause yellowing. In a drugstore or beauty salon find a shampoo that stops yellowing. Clarifying rinses also neutralize yellow. A hairstylist or cosmetologist in a large drugstore can help you find a good product. Why not visit a salon or beauty school and speak to a professional about the yellowing and possibly improving your overall hair color?

Q: *A salon stylist has colored my hair for years. Now I want to save money and do it myself. Any pointers?*

A : It's easy to do. Blond, red or light brown colors are gentle on facial lines. Follow the easy directions. A final cool water rinse closes the pores. Because hair is fragile afterwards, finger comb into place and set. Wait about four to six weeks before recoloring. You might want to call the product's 800 number for more helpful hints.

FASHION

Age is not a factor when selecting clothing. Color, comfort and style lines are.

Q: *How should we go about renewing our wardrobe so we do not look out-of-date?*

A : Your weight and best colors are important considerations. Age is not. Looking good at almost any weight or age is possible. Forget imperfections; focus on your best features. Jackie Onassis developed a memorable style in spite of her H-shaped body.

Renew your appearance with appropriate-for-your-figure hem lengths – not too long if you are petite. Look for nonclinging fabrics and cheerful colors, not dull dark ones.

When you shop for clothing, consider size and color first. Even if it is a designer fashion, you won't wear it if the color is wrong. Because clothing must look better on you than on the hanger, try everything on before a mirror. Look at the front, back and the sides. Does the color enhance your face? Do the style and fabric feel good? It should be comfortable on your figure. Do the sit-down test for slacks, jeans and trousers.

Three great outfits are better than ten mediocre ones. When seasonal colors and fashions do not flatter, pass them up. Stick with your best colors and styles despite fashion dictates. But, something different can be fun. To avoid impulse buying, never shop when you are tired or hungry and always shop when your face and hair are pretty! This simple rule will help you make good decisions.

It is neither vain nor selfish to be creative about our appearance. Looking nifty after fifty is positive action with good psychological and social benefits.

Q: *I wear a size 16/18. What should I do to look as good as I can?*

A : Sixty percent of American women wear size 12 and over. Accept who you are and be aware of your personal goodness. This inner beauty produces outer charm. Learn the art of makeup and adorn your figure with gorgeous colors. Visit plus-size fashion shops. Vertical lines, prints, pinstripes and two-color outfits are good choices and there are many more in these shops including dresses in bold, beautiful colors.

Q : *What style shorts are best for us?*

A : Opt for fluid or crisp fabrics, such as rayon blends and brushed cotton twill rather than stiff denim or clingy knits. Longer shorts that cut off at the knees, or slightly above, cover extra pounds. Let the hem hit at the slimmest part of your inner thighs. Heavy thighs? Wear roomy or A-line shorts or a skort (shorts with a skirtlike front panel). The looseness of a wider, more belled proportion gives the illusion of slimness. Avoid tight waists and bulky pleats that make fabric bulge around the abdomen. Stitched-down pleats are good. Wide hips? Choose flat fronts, no side pockets. Thin legs, thick middle? Wear low-waisted, flat fronts with a straight leg. Improve your legs by wearing hose or a cosmetic cover such as a tanning lotion or Covermark Leg Magic.

Q : *I am excited about my first cruise in the Caribbean. Can you give me some ideas about what I should pack?*

A : Today's fashions for cruises have changed since the Love Boat saga with long dresses and sequined evening gowns. Now most travelers want casual dressing, but check this out with the cruise line. Cruisers choose clothing they can wear after the trip with multiple uses for one item, such as the coverup. Use it over a swimsuit, with a casual outfit, or evening attire. They come in various colors in sheer or knitted fabrics.

Depending upon how long the cruise is, you will want a couple of sundresses, one dressy dress, two pairs of shorts, snappy slacks, and two or three tops. White tee shirts are popular, so are sandals and thongs. Metallic silver or gold sandals can be worn with slacks or shorts and in the evening with sheer hose, a dressy dress or silk pant suit. Accessorize with jewelry in matching metals. You may also want a lightweight jacket for cool evenings and a medium weight shawl when air conditioning is uncomfortably cool. To bask in the sun or swim, take two tummy-control swimsuits, then you have an extra when one is wet.

Scan the clothing you have and try to mix and match. Let apparel be comfortable, colorful, fun to wear in electric or pastel colors. Start shopping several months ahead so you can spread out the expense.

Protect your face and hair from too much sun with a straw hat (secured with ribbon or elastic so it won't blow off), a sun visor, or cap. Take sunscreen SPF 15. If your legs and arms look winter pale, a tanning lotion gives them healthy color. Covermark's *Leg Magic* keeps legs younger-looking under shorts and swimsuit. It covers veins and is waterproof. Follow directions! For attractive hands and sandaled feet, wear nail polish in a luscious color. Cheer up your face with enhancing shades of makeup.

Q: *My problem is finding a bra that looks and feels good. Do they make them for full-figured women who want a youthful figure?*

A : Clothes hang better when we wear a bra that is supportive, comfortable and smooths our form. Sagging bosoms profile the matronly figure that few modern women want. The lingerie section in department stores often has trained fitters who know exactly how a bra should fit. Ask one to help you try on several. You want the correct size around the body, the appropriate cup size and design to shape you the best. Seamless, fiber filled lined cups give the smooth look. Playtex and Warner have these. Women who have arthritis may find the lined Olga bra that closes in front handy. If straps press into your shoulders, look for a bra with wide straps.

Q : *I find nylon hosiery very uncomfortable because they bind. Many of us avoid wearing a dress because of this. Do you have any suggestions?*

A : Get out your lovely dresses and wear hose *without* lycra or control top, such as Penny's economical, good-looking Worthington Sensible Sheers. Hanes has three styles for full figured women in their catalogue, *One Hanes Place.* Their phone number is 800-300-2600. These brands/styles – and there are others – have extra stretch in the waist, hips and thighs for all-day comfort and good fit.

Q : *I have to use crutches or a wheelchair to get around but always want to look as good as I can despite this. Do you have any fashion hints for me?*

A : A woman at one of my presentations was in a wheelchair. Despite the extra effort it takes her to do anything, she looked better than most who attended, and she was smiling! My admiration goes to women in your circumstances who realize the importance of looking their best and by doing that, contribute to the beauty of everyday life. This is positive living, so important after fifty, actually at any age.

Color is your best ally. Try having your shoes, hose and hems in the same color whether you wear a skirt or slacks. Keep pastel and bright colors around the face. Wear ravishing colors in comfortable, roomy but styled tops, example, Chanel jackets, cable sweaters, multicolored vests or jackets. Let sweaters, tee shirts or blouses complement the colors and styles of your jackets and sweaters. Wear darker colors waist down. Skirts that come over the knees are in good taste. Also try ankle length gowns with simple lines and in gorgeous shades. Accessorize with metallic jewelry, pearls and fun pieces. Jewelry brightens and adds a touch of class.

Makeup looks best when the complexion is "polished" with a mask or light skin peel. Apply a quality foundation that gives good coverage. Blush and lip colors are next in importance. Eye makeup beautifies and brings eyes out from behind glasses which tend to hide them.

Hair should be styled soft and flowing with an easy-care cut. If white or grey is depressing, color it. Fashion and makeup provide an opportunity to express your individuality and encourage people to get past the crutches or wheelchair and see you. Use fashions that are enjoyable and fun to wear with simple lines and gorgeous colors. The loveliness of fashion can be yours.

MOTIVATION

Q: *Are there any specific things we should be alert to as we grow older?*

A : Avoid being sedentary or thinking you are "just too tired" or "too old" to do what you know is good for you. This can be the best time of our lives if we try to be all we can be. Maintain a fitness program to have more energy, think clearly, be happier, and sleep sound. A fitness expert and teacher in India, Ramma Bans, said, "The secret of health is exercise. The secret of good looks is exercise. The secret of freezing age is exercise." Moving the bod with exercise or sports invigorates the mind and controls and/or prevents disease. A daily

10-minute warmup combined with a 15-minute walk is a good start.

Let your appearance reflect interest, intelligence and vitality. Attractive light, bright shades favorably affect how we feel and the impression we give. Wearing them expresses a positive and upbeat attitude. Because the hair and skin lose color, use makeup to enliven the face – the focal point of appearance, and consider coloring your hair.

Create a life with enjoyment, adventure and personal challenge. Fight to keep a positive attitude. Abandon critical, depressing thoughts and never stop learning.

Q : *I'm afraid my "beauty," vigor and enthusiasm will go downhill when I retire because I won't have a routine or much money. Can you give me words of encouragement?*

A : George Burns wrote in one of his books that the greatest danger of retirement is we start to practice being old – posture slumps, feet shuffle, appearance is so-so, learning stops, and thinking becomes self-centered. When people reposition their activities and plan their life, retirement blossoms into a fulfilling experience. History records people who have done this successfully. Thousands are doing it now.

Design a retirement plan similar to this:
• Service and work are important for mental health.
• Caring about appearance is not egotistical; it is unselfish self-care and affects attitude. You may not need as many clothes. Excellent skin care products and cosmetics are available in drugstores.
• Cut health costs and increase energy by eating healthy, staying fit and banishing destructive habits. This means eating

fruits, vegetables, drinking more water (don't wait till you're thirsty!) and integrating exercise that you enjoy into *every* week.

- Retain an ongoing education program. Stimulate your mind with classes, good books, hobbies, creating and recreating.
- Make new friends, stay involved and you'll be healthier. True friends are angels who help, inspire, encourage, and are fun. Finally, give to the world the beauty of your smile and good will.
- Plan something special every day.

Many of us are more attractive and interesting in the older years than in the younger ones.

Q: *I cry every night since I was diagnosed with breast cancer. What helps?*

A : Read Sue Buchanan's book *Love, Laughter and A High Disregard for Statistics, surviving breast cancer with your sense of humor and your sexuality intact* (Thomas Nelson Publishers, Nashville, TN). Buchanan went through what you are. Her experience and fortitude are an inspiration. Call Y-ME (800) 221-2141 and talk to someone who understands. Do not isolate yourself. Stay busy and involved. Working is a lifesaver and support groups offer understanding, camaraderie and fun, too. Stay physically active – walking around a park, gentle stretch exercises and exercises your doctor recommends – helps to erase the blues. Wear makeup and cheerful colors in clothing. Wearing color on face and figure will lift your spirits.

Q : *At 80, can I still look like a winner?*

A : If you have the desire and energy, yes. One of the grandest women I ever met attended one of my makeup classes. She was 81and wanted to learn the latest techniques, because, she said, it's never too late to learn. A 90 year old woman called me from Oregon requesting my book, *Look Like A Winner After 50,* because she needed some new tips!

Q : *My children pity me because I am now a widow. Maybe if I looked better, it would lessen the pity. What do you think?*

A : After a certain age, most of us start to think of ourselves as old and people pick up on that. If we don't want to be treated as a sad, older person, we have to reprogram our thinking, spruce up our appearance, and uplift our attitude. Too often people attach their idea of 50, 60, 70, whatever, to us. They do not realize how independent, adventurous, enterprising, observant and smart we are!

Appearance isn't everything but it plays a big part in the way people treat us. Wear makeup, redo your hair, wear stylish clothing in flattering colors. Stand tall! Good posture gives you an upbeat persona and everything looks better. Tune in to your inner vitality and beauty, which are ageless.

New products and fashions will be flooding the market to keep us looking like the special women we are. Watch for them in your newspapers and women's magazines.

CHAPTER 6

Create a life you are happy living!

Your life is up to you. Life provides the canvas; you do the painting.
– Author Unknown

When we withdraw our fixation on the age number, we can rejuvenate our lives. One woman said, "Find an age you like and stay with it." Barbara Walters said in a TV interview that life is constant growth. This is the "grow young" philosophy. During a group hike in the Rocky Mountains, we came to a lake and sat on boulders beneath the snow-topped peaks to have our lunch. One woman said she was 68 and so glad she made it that far. A man piped in and said he was 73 and felt like going on another five miles. Another woman squirmed around and finally asked impatiently, "Why are we always talking about how old we are? Is that all we can talk about? Is our age some kind of merit badge?"

During interviews, they always ask my age. It's an identifying hook. I have found that it's better to say I'm over 60 because when I give the number they start to talk louder and slower! Age, a natural happening, is nothing to be ashamed of or bragged about. However, too often, public opinion identifies age with *its concept* of what being old is like. It is governed by general stereotypes about aging, such as diminishing health, intelligence and vitality, that no longer apply. For proof, look at the senior golf tournaments and Senior Olympics occurring in many states. In addition to this, women over 50 are practicing their professions, starting businesses, writing and publishing books, painting and exhibiting their works of art, helping to rear grandchildren – the list goes on and on.

Dwelling on the age number can be devitalizing. As old fashioned as it may seem, it is better in most circumstances to keep it private and cease being obsessed by it. Many of us do not look, act or think like a particular age. Often, there is a young woman inside who is poised for fun or a caring woman whose compassion knows no bounds.

Because of the stigma against elders in the United States, some women hide their age or pretend to be younger. This indicates a false sense of quality and an insecurity. We seem to be obsessed with the age number. Just as ethnicity, religion and politics color the opinion of an individual, so does age. These identifications describe only a very small part of the complex and multifaceted individual. When we stop imitating the outdated mannerisms of the elderly during previous generations, age discrimination may lessen. Age is far from being a definitive measure. There are young women who are mature, talented and skilled beyond their years. On the other hand, there are people in their 60s who are still waiting to grow up!

In his book, *Wellness and Health Promotion for the Elderly*, Ken Dychtwalk, Ph.D. wrote that we have traveled more places, read more books and magazines, met more people, and lived longer than any previous cohort in world history. We are part of a powerful "elderculture."

Modern lifestyles open the way to celebrate peace of mind and body and satisfying social experiences. The MacArthur Foundation Research on Aging in America published the results of a 10-year study of several thousand men and women in the book, *Successful Aging*. They found that *lifestyle choices – more than genes – determine how well and how long we live*. The best program for our life includes certain guidelines emphasized in the study, namely:

- Healthy habits, such as no smoking, a sensible diet and regular physical exercise;
- Lifelong education to maintain and cultivate an active mind;
- Social relationships, especially friends "to talk things over with."

The study revealed that by stimulating our mental functions, we are more likely to retain the physical functions. We don't have to fit into conventional patterns. By reinventing, recreating and redefining our life to produce happiness, we can have amazing results.

Let your creative juices flow! Creativity, a source for solutions and a gift from the Creator, is an incomparable, life-giving force. It has a biochemical significance in the body, producing vital brain impulses that contribute strongly to well-being.

Your fountain of creativity is unlimited, unending, and always available. It is not trivial. *To the imposed limits of later years, creativity can be our most profound response. It opens the tap for individual expression and the satisfaction that it evolves.* We can dip into this reservoir any time. Think of the great works, even the not-so-great ones, that have given continuing enjoyment to millions for millenniums. Creativity is not reserved for a few great ones. It is for the everyday woman. We have to turn it on. Before we can see in a dark room, we have to turn on the light – take action.

Curiosity is sister to creativity. Pursue your quest! The yen for knowledge, expression, experimentation and discovery accompanies creativity. Don't let procrastination or doubt undermine your faith and belief in the creative force within you. The only limitations are the ones you accept. Have you heard of the armless people who paint pictures holding the brush in their toes or in their teeth? Their work is remarkable.

It is humbling to think of the painstaking patience they have to learn the method, let alone produce salable art.

It takes creativity to cook a delicious meal, cultivate a garden, knit a sweater, plan a business meeting, operate a business, conduct an orchestra or choir, prepare a party, do scientific research, teach in a class, design buildings and bridges, organize, manage, etc. The avenues for it are infinite.

Visualization or mental imagery is a technique to stimulate creativity and relieve the stress, that can block the flow of ideas. It is like a mental vacation that you can take any time to calm your mind. Simply, find a quiet place where you can sit comfortably. Close your eyes, take a couple of deep breaths. In your mind's eye, take yourself to a peaceful, happy scene – a beautiful meadow filled with wildflowers, a sunny beach with the roar of ocean waves, or a happy scene from your childhood. Now, put yourself in the picture. Wade in the ocean, feel and smell the salt water, or if you are in the meadow, smell the grass and flowers, feel the brush of a breeze against your cheek or the gentle grass against your legs, the warm sun on your face. Your mind and body will begin to respond as if you were actually there. The stress and pressure will float away and you will smile with contentment.

You can also use visualization to solve problems. Visualize the situation or project. See yourself or the people involved and visualize a successful solution. Let the solution with its components flow naturally without any force. Everything in this scene is working harmoniously with no glitches. Keep it as peaceful as the meadow with the spring breezes. Try imaging for 10 to 15 minutes whenever you need refreshment. This is good stimulation for your imagination.

Dr. Maxwell Maltz, renowned plastic surgeon and author of *Psycho-Cybernetics*, called this silent space the quiet room within, a place where we can find peace and solutions. This is a space we can design to suit our need of the moment.

WAYS TO STIMULATE CREATIVITY

- Emancipate yourself from limiting, preconceived notions about yourself and longevity.
- Concentrate and visualize. Silence, solitude and focused thought spawn creative ideas.
- Never criticize or squelch the first bubbling of creative ideas. Write them down and let them run the course before you refine.
- When you are facing a dead end, do something physically vigorous to destress.
- When the creative process is working, listen to your hunches.
- Saturate your conscious and subconscious mind in the genre you are interested in. If it is music, listen to good music. If poetry, read good poetry. If art, go regularly to art museums and exhibits to view and sketch, and so on.
- Recreate the good activities from youth that made you happy.
- Visit your library or bookstore and look up books or audio tapes in an area of interest.
- Research related subjects.
- Read the works of great thinkers of today and yesterday. A librarian can guide you. Peruse the bibliography of this book for further helpful reading.
- Scan or read newspapers and magazines to stay current on local, national and international affairs. Analyze and form an opinion.
- Improve your ability to study, learn and apply.
- Exercise discrimination. Question everything.
- Playing relaxes the mind, removes tension that obstructs the free flow of thought. Playing provides fun and joy. We need this! Just as we need to tilt to the lighter side. Plato said, "Life must be lived as play."

- To remove blocks, learn a relaxation technique. It can be yoga, deep breathing, meditation, or walking.
- Have an ongoing self-education program. Some universities and colleges have a program for people over 65 allowing them to sit in classes at little or no expense. Or, do it on your own.
- Negative thinking stultifies. Expose it and, if necessary, express it when relationships are involved. Be creative and harmoniously resolve the discord.
- Never dwell on critical self-thought. Dwell on solutions.
- Let bad memories fade away. They take up thought space that can be used constructively.
- Only what is going on now is important. How we think now determines the quality of the future.
- Complaining snuffs out creativity. Shut it off and regenerate your thinking.

Depression may not be recognized. A woman who had lost a loved one told her doctor she had no interest in anything, not even eating. After discussing her daily activities, the doctor shocked her by saying, "You have gone from sadness to depression. We can start treating and curing it." She had not recognized her dark feelings as depression. By following the treatment her doctor advised – a change in diet, medication and exercise – she snapped out of it. Most depression improves significantly with treatment and is sometimes caused by a chemical imbalance. It has been called the "Great Masquerader" because it is frequently not identified and often misdiagnosed.

Persistent sadness, anxiety or "empty" moods are not part of normal aging. Depression is not age-related. However, health problems, disability and social isolation increase its occurrence. Five or more of the following symptoms for two weeks or longer suggest depression:

Sad moods most of the day, nearly every day.
Little interest in daily activities.
Significant changes in weight or appetite.
Trouble sleeping or sleeping too much.
Hyperactive or inactive.
Fatigue or lack of energy.
Anxiety, constant worrying.
Feelings of worthlessness, guilt, pessimism or hopelessness.
Problems with thinking, concentrating or making decisions.
Aches, pains and sexual problems.
Changes in appetite and significant weight loss or gain.
Recurring thoughts of death or suicide.

The fact that many celebrities have openly admitted to being treated for depression has made it easier for individuals to recognize symptoms and seek help. Art Linkletter advised combating depression by believing in a higher power and omnipresent goodness, staying socially active, participating in community activities and exercise. These destress the mind.

Whenever possible, associate with people who think progressively, cheerfully, enthusiastically – the doers and constructive thinkers. This preserves our mental and physical health. Avoid negators and killjoys – unpleasant, self-centered people who tend to drag us down. Misery can be self-imposed or caused by the unconscious or conscious actions of others. If someone accidentally grabbed a hot poker, would you say, "Hold it"? Or, would you scream, "DROP IT, NOW!" Hurtful experiences are like hot pokers. We have to release them in order for healing to begin. True healing comes when there is a righteous, spiritual lift that enables us to forgive, if the fault is not ours, or reform, if it is.

A longtime friend from my high school days diagnosed herself as depressed and decided to read all of Norman Vincent Peale's books. She became more alert to her thoughts and made every effort to keep them occupied with the inspiring ideas in these books. Over a period of several months, she healed herself. The result was a more wholesome approach to everyday life. Over time she created a strong foundation. It gave her the inner fortitude and intelligence to meet all adverse situations constructively rather than resorting to self-pity and helplessness. Instead of rehearsing problems she dealt with them and let them go. However, she said positive thinking is something she has to work at all the time, or it can get away from you. It isn't always easy but it is better than staying sad.

The media can be a monster! Spending hours sitting mindlessly in front of a TV watching hopeless human scenarios and depressing news doesn't help us. Occasionally, viewers may even ask themselves, "Why am I watching this? It's so demoralizing." Listening frequently to the radio can have the same effect. We all know about the junk-food for the mind found on commercial TV. On the other hand, there are excellent programs such as newscasts, good quality drama and comedy, operas, concerts, and documentaries that broaden our horizon.

Dr. Art Ulene in his address to the 1997 AARP convention implored his listeners to take charge of their health and quality of life. He said the risk of obesity is directly related to the amount of TV a person watches and recommended limiting it to one hour a day.

Some women would be a lot more active, a lot more interesting if their mind and sensibilities were not numbed by excess television. By substituting fitness activity, reading, working, hobbies, creative pursuits, or social work, they might be surprised at how their attitude improves.

Recent studies show that constantly cruising the internet increases loneliness. The same can be said for all media. The conclusion is that repetitive behavior without diversity can lead to bordom, loneliness and depression. We need to be with friends, family and people in general, combined with a program of planned activities, to defeat unhappiness.

Caregivers, give yourself a break! While I was still working 40 hours a week in the corporate world, I brought my 80 year old aunt to live with me in my condo because she was left without a home. After six months I consulted a gerontologist in a nearby hospital. She surprised me by saying, "If you go on as you are, you'll die before she does. She needs to be with other old people who like listening to the same stories and enjoy them every time. You need a life." When I followed her advice and placed my aunt in a home setting with like-minded women, she was happier because she was not alone during the day. My life became more normal, too.

A reader of my *Beauty Beyond 50* column called me about a makeup question that led to another matter that troubled her. She was overweight, wanted to get back in shape, and was dissatisfied with herself. She told me her 90 year old mother lived with her. Consequently, she was home all the time and getting fatter and fatter. She did not want to take diet pills and had a treadmill but never used it. I told her to get a regular sitter for her mom so she could get out of the house more. Then, take fitness classes and participate in the social activities at her senior, community center, athletic club or church.

She also needed the advice of a gerontologist on caring not only for her mother but also reinforcement for herself. Support groups for caregivers offer opportunities to exchange ideas on coping with the frustrations of overwhelming day-to-day responsibilities. The gerontologist departments of local hospitals have referrals to various support groups. Talking it over with a professional counselor and a support group is encouraging and provides helpful community resources.

Caregivers must give equal time to their own welfare so they have the necessary mental and physical strength. This is not selfish because neglecting health and well-being saps energy. By giving sufficient time to their own personal welfare, caregivers can more graciously take care of other responsibilities. They should not feel guilty about scheduling time to maintain social ties, relax, pursue hobbies and other activities. They need a refresher. Be honest about your needs with family members and ask for help when necessary.

A caregiver needs to: (1) Create a schedule of activities that strengthens, releases stress, and is enjoyable. (2) Give herself a pep talk several times a day. (3) Eliminate belittling self-talk. Athough the role of a caregiver is extremely difficult, coping strategies provide relief.

Just do it! We can't depend on other people to make our life click. It is deadly to succumb to apathy, laziness or a feeling of helplessness. Sometimes we have to force ourselves to do what is good for us. Be creative and use the "stick and carrot" method. We have to exercise our will and do what is beneficial. Doing it brightens our day. We feel like conquerors! We are, because we defeated the green dragon of procrastination that prevents progress! Satisfaction in life is worth every battle it takes. Then, reward yourself with a special treat. Rewarding ourselves becomes part of the fun of doing what we truly need to do.

"I want to find a job." Working with people toward a common goal is very satisfying for all ages. Some kind of work is imperative for self-worth. Work is an opportunity to be with people, to serve, to help, to grow, to feel needed and appreciated.

Positive attitudes make us desirable candidates for employment. For example, how do you respond to new ideas?

With an open mind? "Sure, let's try it." Or, do you instantly think, "It's never been done like that, so why change?" The desirable attitude is to be always willing to try a new approach to see if it improves a given situation. No employer needs us if we are unwilling to learn and experiment with new ideas.

Some managers do not want older people around no matter how pleasant, willing, or skillful they are. Mature candidates may remind them of a close relative whose attitude was dictatorial and superior, who looked at them as lesser beings. That can't be helped, and we cannot change them. We can move on *with positive expectancy* to find our niche.

A basic formula for finding employment is:
- Before the interview, decide how you can help the employer and at the right time, express it.
- Have the required expertise.
- Smile and be friendly. Look attractive not just clean. Wear attractive color on face and figure.
- Be flexible and a keen listener.
- Give opinions only when asked.
- Remember, every job requires a different approach. Understand the business so you have the right one.
- Never cave in to discouragement.

If a woman has difficulty fitting into today's market or has no desire to, she can start her own business or do volunteer work. Strong desire and persistence open doors.

Grow young! The big three – eating healthy, staying fit and updating appearance – make it possible. Add to this positive thinking/attitude and work/service and you have the recipe for the age-free life. Old stereotypes are fading away as science and education reveal health-giving ways to live happily after 50.

It is up to each individual to plant the seeds that will grow their life into one that is happy. Relegate old thoughts, old hurts, old bad memories to the background. Visualize the way you want your life. Water your visions daily with new ideas until they bloom in your garden of life, free from the weeds of despair, idleness and boredom.

During every decade, we can create new purpose. Those who accept age as just another period of development continue to use their own mix of energies and abilities to enrich their life. Artistic, scientific, commercial, athletic, or literary achievements do not always peak in youth. Women who have juggled career, marriage, and family are used to change and impermanence. They generally adapt well to the transition after 50. But, those who have played rigid roles and think of change as fraught with problems are likely to have trouble handling it.

Age is one of many transitions in life. When we use the "grow young" philosophy – embodied in the big three, we make the transitions after 50 with aplomb. After our reproductive prime, we can still experience exhilarating new successes by having ongoing goals and purposes. Not rigid ones, but goals that can be modified or discarded and new ones adopted. Flexibility is important; it offers choices. Rigidity causes stress and anxiety. Pursuing activities that challenge our mental and physical abilities has numerous advantages.

Growing young is practical. Deteriorations of memory, intelligence, productivity and ability are not inevitable. Decline sets in when we submit to the general belief about aging and start to practice being old instead of copying the modalities of vital peers. Self-engendered limitations can block our ability and talent. We can remain adamant like a fossil or grow like a plant. The years after 50 can be a time for rebirth that starts with discovering our authentic, our true self. That self often thrives in satisfying work and complex purposes that demand continual mindfulness.

Leaping from the negative to the positive, plus the learning process – whether it's a skill, game or science – develops brain power. Any energetic and creative activity makes new brain connections called dendrites. Specifically, dendrites are thin, fiber-like extensions in the brain's nerve cells that can grow and create more brain connections for us to use. The process can reverse deterioration. When the brain is kept active, dendrites can continue to increase until the end of life. This is one scientific conclusion that makes growing young now possible. An example of this is learning and using a computer. It sharpens the brain and reasoning processes. The brain is unbelievably plastic, responding positively to challenging actions of both the mind and body.

Phyllis Whitney, author of 33 romantic suspense novels and one of the world's best selling authors, said her books written in later years were better than the ones written when she was younger, and her health is better now, too. She believes in daily physical exercise and that we can always learn new ways. Sharing, helping and giving must be part of living, she notes. We always get back what we give.

In one of her talks, Eleanor Roosevelt advocated the ability to be curious, to feel the flow of new ideas, and the unselfishness to think of others so that we never grow old or bored. Life expands when we investigate new interests – organizations that need volunteers, learn new hobbies, add words to our vocabulary, read books in different genres, take classes, join in the activities of recreation or senior centers, meet new people, converse on varied topics, invent, create, and so on. You may have a hidden talent you haven't explored.

Eisenhower, Churchill and Grandma Moses found their talent for painting late in life. Lesser known people are doing the same every day. One grandmother in a suburban community had a reputation for baking delicious breads and cookies. She needed some extra money and, since so many friends raved about her treats, she started taking orders during the November and December holidays. The word got around and after a couple years, she hired two women to help her.

However, life always holds the possibility of failure. After all, failure is the other side of success. Our years of experience have surely given us the resiliency to use failure as a springboard to bounce back. Failures precede all shining successes. When we look at failure as a lesson to be learned, greater achievement occurs. The struggle is important because the climb to the summit is as important as the view from the top. There are thousands of examples of this. Look what Jimmy Carter has done since his presidency, building communities in the needy areas of the world. Look at Angela Lansbury's amazing acting career. In 1997 when she was in her 70s, she received the Screen Guild's Lifetime Achievement award. As she held the award, she exclaimed, "I am galvanized to strike out for new goals!"

At 72, ex-President George Bush fulfilled a longheld dream to repeat the parachute leap he made in WW II when he was injured. He jumped 12,500 feet and was bursting with joy when he landed. He is one of the thousands who prove we can still be frisky after fifty. Earlier in this century, Helen Keller, deaf and blind, overcame daunting obstacles and became an international lecturer and wrote several books including *The Story of My Life*. She said, "I seldom think about my limitations, and they never make me sad. Perhaps there is just a touch of yearning at times; but it is vague, like a breeze among flowers."

> *If you fall down seven times,*
> *get up eight.*
>
> *Old Japanese philosopher*

Drifting along in mindlessness leads to oldness and an easy road to depression, but mindful involvement is rejuvenating. Taking control and developing the strong thought that conquers moods and germinates the "can do" attitude is another definition of growing young. A planned schedule that includes work/service, fitness, creativity and a spiritual quest is essential to growing young. All of the components bless our being. Each part of such a schedule inspires goals. They can be mini – walking in a park ten minutes every other day, or maxi – painting pictures and exhibiting them.

The following are do's and don'ts to finding a life you are happy living:

DON'TS

Don't be a doormat for someone's bossiness or frustrations.

Don't be obsessed with past bad memories.

Don't waste time and thought on things you can't change.

Don't blame yourself when you have a setback. Quickly ask, what can I learn from this?

Don't let anyone make you feel defeated.

Don't digest thought-poisons, such as gossip and destructive criticism.

Don't be a reformer. Accept human differences.

Don't let tradition paralyze your mind.

Don't argue about trivial things. Is it really worth the discomfort of disagreement? Why not just agree to disagree?

DO'S for yourself:

Act happy even when you may not feel it. Soon, you will.

Going and doing it alone is okay, often better.

Learn how to supercharge yourself – physically, mentally, spiritually.

Look good on the outside; you'll feel better on the inside.

Find the good side in every situation and whip discouragement.

Do what you fear and fear disappears. Risks are okay.

Action increases confidence and nullifies fear. Inaction destroys confidence and strengthens fear.

Think in terms of doing it now. Be an "I'll-do-it-now" person.

Believe you can do what's good for you.

Practice being the kind of person you like.

Get plenty of psychological sunshine in new groups and new things to do. Look for laughs!

Always ask yourself, "How can I do better?"

Conquer the crime of self-depreciation. You're better than you think.

Make a supreme effort to deposit only positive thoughts in your memory bank.

Discipline yourself to remember.

Stretch your vision. See new value to people and *yourself.*

Let commitment, determination and integrity inspire you to persist.

Write down your thoughts, anxieties and inspirations in a spiral notebook. Forget grammar and syntax, just get the words down. We straighten out our thinking, release pent-up emotions and retain important impressions when we put them on paper.

Speak into a tape recorder and express your troubles and worries. You will sleep better.

Do something special for your mate. No mate? Do it for yourself, especially around the holidays.

DO'S for relationships:

Take the initiative in building friendships. Friends have double value now. One good friend is often more important than family members.

Train yourself to remember names.

Think positive about people if you want positive results. Look for qualities to admire.

Be generous in conversation and make eye contact. Listen and encourage others to talk.

Use words that breathe hope, happiness, and pleasure; avoid images of failure, defeat, pettiness.

Be courteous and appreciative; it makes people feel better...and you, too.

Recall unpleasant events or situations only for the purpose of correcting or healing.

Stretch your mind and try to understand people of different cultural and social interests.

A bird can soar because
he takes himself lightly.

(Calligraph on a Japanese drawing
in a seniors art exhibit.)

Spread your wings and fly! Yes, metaphysically, but also travel-wise. Travel stimulates new ways of thinking about people, cultures, societies and ourselves. It takes body and mind on a refreshing jaunt to new adventures and give us new perspectives about people, our country and nations. More and more women are traveling alone or with another woman when a male companion is not available. It is far better to do it alone than to forgo the travel adventure.

Dorothy Maroncelli, retired travel agent and award-winning Certified Travel Counselor, wrote *Britain on Your Own* for single people who want to travel. She says, "Solo travel can be a joy for today's vital, interested-in-everything, 50-plus woman. Design a travel plan to fit your personal requirements. Pack your bag and camera, set off with élan, and start to gather memories to treasure." And, here's a bonus for you! If you have doubts, Dorothy can share her experience with you. Write to her at West Wind Books, P.O. Box 246, Dundee, MN 55019.

Traveling solo – whether "suddenly single" because of death or divorce, or single by choice is rewarding when your objectives, each day's events are outlined, and you are open to exchanging ideas with the people you meet. Savvy travelers recommend one carry-on bag on wheels and another shoulder bag – even for three weeks.

For an exciting, outdoor or cultural vacation, investigate the itineraries of Explorations in Travel, group travel arrangements for women over 40. The activities are geared for a range of skill levels, so even if you've never been skiing, hiking, canoeing or rafting before, you can join the group without hesitation. Open the door of opportunity to discover a great new past-time, adventure and new friends. Here's a sampling of their guided trips: hiking and canoeing in Vermont, Windjammer sailing in Maine, skiing in Minnesota, walking in the French Pyrenees, sailing the Greek Islands, hiking in New Zealand. Attendees have written: "I left renewed, inspired and with a feeling of empowerment."... "I'm still flying high. Such a rewarding and enriching experience for me."..."[You] did a super job of making me feel that anything was possible." Information is available from Explorations in Travel, 275 Jacksonville Stage Road, Brattleboro, VT 05301, phone (802) 257-0152.

How you live the second half of life is the example you leave for friends and relatives who follow you. Either they will realize the empowerment of the years after 50 or the lethargy and boredom. As we move into an unknown future, we leave an example for future generations. Dr. Maxwell Maltz wrote in his best selling book, Psycho-Cybernetics, that if you have had strong religious beliefs, now is the time to emphatically live them, not just mouth them. The benefits are twofold – for yourself and for others.

The word 'enthusiasm' comes from the Greek word *enthousiasmos* which means "'the God within you." Enthusiasm is faith in action. A life lived with enthusiasm is one lived well. We don't have to act old by complaining, gossiping or using our age as an excuse. We can refuse to carry negativity because it broadcasts itself. We can throw away ill feelings because they make us feel unhappy, and isn't it a good time to mend the fences of time? We can still think and act youthfully and creatively, and accept challenges. We can smile and laugh without fear of wrinkles, because in truth they help prevent them.

Creativity, a good attitude, healthy eating, staying fit and a nifty appearance are the recipes to growing young. But, to be obsessed with any of these is to miss the mark. It is like knowing how to recite inspiring words but ignoring the meaning, or, playing music perfectly without the dynamics. Keep life simple! Do what is necessary, then forget the process. Enjoy the people, the scenery surrounding you, the activity, the world, as well as the inner silence where truly the loving life begins.

References

Chapter 1

Anatomy of An Illness by Norman Cousins. 1979, pages 40 and 87.

Chapter 2

<u>Books:</u>

Looneyspoons, Low-Fat foods made Fun! by Janey & Greta Podleski. What a joy it is to just peruse this "cook book" and read its tips on *Show Me the 'Weigh'* (zapping fat), *Cooking 101, D.I.E.T* (Dangerously Inadvisable Eating Tactics), *Gotta Move It* (physical activity) let alone its healthy-eating/tasty recipes, jokes and cartoons!

Stay Young the Melatonin Way by Steven J. Bock, M.D. and Michael Boyette. This is an easy-to-read and understand text with a plan for better health and longer life.

Brain Builders, Richard Leviton. A highly recommended book that offers specific brain exercises and maintenance for the "age-proof mind."

<u>Newsletters:</u>

The Wellness Nutrition Counter by Sheldon Margen, M.D. and the Editors of the University of California-Berkeley Wellness Letter, a guide to complete nutritional information and analysis of over 6,000 foods and products, 1-904-445-6414.

UC Berkeley Wellness Letter, 1-904-445-6414, a popular

newsletter about nutrition, fitness, and stress management. Oct. 1997; Jan., Feb., Apr., Aug., Sept. 1998.

Harvard Women's Health Watch, 1-800-829-5921, a newsletter covering all of women's health issues. Jan. 1998 (vitamin D), July 1998
Magazine: Modern Maturity, A Call for Calcium, March-April, 1998

The National Institute on Aging Information Center has a list of free publications on a variety of topics. 800-222-2225, P.O. Box 8057, Gaithersburg, MD 20898-8057.

Chapter 3

Physical Activity and Health, A Report of the Surgeon General, July 1996. Superintendent of Documents, P.O. Box 371954, Pittsburgh, PA 15250-7954, Order Code No. 7895, published by the U.S. Department of Health and Resources.

Books:
Biomarkers, The 10 Determinants of Aging You can Control by William Evans, Ph.D. and Irwin H. Roseberg, M.D. with Jacqueline Thompson, A medically proven program that can slow down the aging process and add renewed strength and vitality to your life – no matter what your age!
Conquering Heart Disease, New Ways to Live Well without Drugs or Surgery by Harvey B. Simon, M.D., Harvard Medical School
Hooked on Exercise by Doctors Rebecca Prussin, Philip Harvey and Theresa DiGeronimo
Walking Medicine by Gary Yanker & Kathy Burton with a

team of 50 medical experts The lifetime guide to
preventive & therapeutic exercise walking programs
The New Yoga for People Over 50 by Suza Francina
A comprehensive guide for midlife and older beginners
The Complete Book of Thai Chi by Steward McFarlane

Newsletters:
University of California-Berkeley Wellness Letter, Jan. 1998
So Young!, Dedicated to a youthful body, mind & spirit,
published by Anti-Aging Press, Inc., P.O. Box 141489,
Coral Gables, FL 33114, Julia Busch, Editor
Harvard Women's Health Watch, Aug. 1996, Nov. 1997, April
1998

Senior newspapers, particularly *The Senior News* - Dundee,
Illinois; *Senior Times* - Kalamazoo, MI; *Mature Living* -
Toledo, OH; *Get Up & Go!* - Salem, OR; *Leisure Living* -
Baltimore, MD; *Senior Messenger* - Vancouver, WA;
Senior Beacon - Buffalo, NY; *Valley Messenger* - Yucaipa,
CA
The New York Times, June 1993

The American College of Sports Medicine and other national
organizations continually circulate information recom-
mending physical activity for people over 50.

Chapter 4

Books:
Look Like A Winner After 50 with Care, Color & Style, 3rd
edition by Jo Peddicord, 1997 Denver, Colorado: Golden
Aspen Publishing. Detailed how-tos with illustrations
and photos for all women past midlife covering the total
image i.e. color, makeup, hands, hair, erasing the

wrinkles, fashion for different body types and camouflaging, even teeth.

Beauty Wisdom by Bharti Vyas with Claire Haggard. 1997. London: Thorsons, 1997. This book has good ideas for women over 50, although it seems to be addressing primarily younger women.

Magazines:

MORE for active women over 40. For more information call toll-free 888-699-4036.

Good Housekeeping, McCall's. Adapt the styles and makeup you see on younger women to your preference and style.

Chapter 6

Golden Life Senior Newspaper, Florence, SC, August 1998.

Books:

Successful Aging by John W. Rowe, M.D. and Robert L. Kahn, Ph.D., Pantheon Books. The authors are two of the researchers in the MacArthur Foundation Research Network.

Anatomy of An Illness by Norman Cousins. 1979.

The Roosevelts, American Aristocrats by Allen Churchill.

The Courage to Grow Old by Phillip L. Berman, Ballantine Books: New York, 1989.

Pscho-Cybernetics, Maltz, Maxwell, M.D., F.I.C.S., Simon and Schuster: New York, 1960. A new way to get more living out of life. Based on an amazing new scientific innovation, this simple yet practical "new way of life" can be the most important influence in your life!

Harvard Women's Health Watch Newsletter, Jan. 1998.

Bibliography

Books are best friends.

These books will help you to expand upon feeling nifty after 50 and to realize the advantages to "growing young."

Bock, Steven J., M.D. & Michael Boyette. 1995. *Stay Young the Melatonin Way*, Dutton: New York City.

Cameron, Julia, Mark Bryan. 1992. *The Artist's Way*, New York City: G.P. Putnam. A course in discovering and recovering your creative self, a spiritual path to higher creativity.

Canfield, Jack and Mark Victor Hansen. 1993. *Chicken Soup for the Soul*, Dearfield Beach, FL: Health Communications, Inc. 101 stories by well-known and unknown thinkers to open the heart and rekindle the spirit.

Cousins, Norman. 1979. *Anatomy of An Illness*, W.W. Norton & Company: New York City. This is an oustanding book written for the everyday person and anyone who doubts the power of a positive attitude. Cousins also wrote *Head First, The Biology of Hope*.

Evans, Ph.D, William and Irwin H. Rosenberg, M.D. with Jacqueline Thompson. 1991. *Biomarkers, The 10 Determinants of Aging You Can Control*, New York City: Simon & Schuster.

Fisher, Mark. 1990. *The Instant Millionaire*, Novato, CA: New World Library. A tale of wisdom and wealth.

Fisher, Mark and Marc Allen. 1990. *How to Think Like A Millionaire*, Novato, CA: New World Library.

Friedan, Betty. 1993. *The Fountain of Age*, New York City: Simon & Schuster. An indepth and rewarding read with scientific evidence denouncing the stereotypes of aging.

Helmstetter, Shad. 1990. *Finding the Fountain of Youth Inside Yourself*, New York City: Pocket Books,a division of Simon & Schuster Inc. Overflowing with ways to start you thinking right and overcoming old, outdated ideas.

Heuts, Olivier. 1997. *It's Never Too Late to Look & Feel Younger Through Exercise*, Greenport, NY: Pilot Books.

Hill, Napoleon. 1979. *The Law of Success*, Chicago, IL: Success Unlimited, Inc.

Hopkins, Patricia and Sherry Anderson. 1991. *The Feminine Face of God: The Unfolding of the Sacred in Women*, New York City: Bantam Books, a division of Bantam Doubleday Dell Publishing Group, Inc. 1991.

Jampolsky, M.D., Gerald G. 1983. *Teach Only Love*, New York City: Bantam Books. He is also the author of *Love is Letting Go of Fear*.

Leviton, Richard. 1995. *Brain Builders*, New York City: Parker.

Larson, Earnie. 1992. *From Anger to Forgiveness*, New York City: Ballantine Books.

Margen, M.D. Sheldon and Editors of the University of California at Berkeley Wellness Letter, 1997. *The Wellness Nutrition Counter*, New York, NY: Rebus, Inc., 1997. Data about a healthy diet, vitamins and minerals, general foods and brands.

Maroncelli, Dorothy. 1997, *Britain on Your Own, A Guide for Single Mature Travelers*, Dundas, MN: West Wind Books.

Nelson, Ph.D, Miriam E. 1998. *Strong Women Stay Young*, New York City: Bantam. A scientifically proven strength-training program.

Paffenbarger, Dr. Ralph S., Eric Olsen. 1996. *LifeFit: An Effective Exercise Program for Optimal Health and a Longer Life*, Champaign, IL: Human Kinectics

Peale, Norman Vincent. 1996. *Positive Imaging*, New York City: Fawcett Crest

Podleski, Janet & Greta, 1997, *Looneyspoons*, Fairfield, IA: Granet Publishing Inc.

Schwartz, Ph.D, David Joseph. 1959. *The Magic of Thinking Big*, Englewood Cliffs, NJ: Prentice-Hall, Inc.

Sher, Barbara, Annie Gottlief. 1979. *Wishcraft How to Get What You Really Want*, New York City: Ballantine Books.

Siegel, M.D., Bernie S. 1986. *Love, Medicine & Miracles Lessons Learned About Self-Healing from a Surgeon's Experience with Exceptional Patients*, New York City: Harper & Row

Smithsonian Institution. 1981. *The, Fire of Life, The Smithsonian Book of the Sun*, Washington D.C.: Smithsonian Books.

Syza, Francina. 1997. *The New Yoga for People Over 50, A Comprehensive Guide for Midlife & Older Beginners*, Deerfield Beach, FL: Health Communications, Inc. Reveals the practicability of yoga for us folks.

Ward, Susan Winter. 1994. *Yoga for the Young at Heart, Gentle Stretching Exercises for Seniors*, Santa Barbara, CA: Capra Press (P.O.Box 2068, Santa Barbara, CA 93120 or 800-558-9642) Get the feeling of your body "flowing" from one exercise to another. An energizing plan for beginners and the more experienced. An audio is also available.

Warner, Carolyn. 1992. *The Last Word, a Treasury of Women's Quotes*, New Jersey: Prentice Hall.

Yanker, Gary, Kathy Burton with a tem of 50 medical experts. 1990. *Walking Medicine*, New York City: McGraw-Hill, Inc.

Yogananda, Parmahansa. 1988. *Where There Is Light*, Self Realization Fellowship: Los Angeles, CA. Practical, spiritual counsel for meeting everyday challenges.

Index

More Publications
by Jo Peddicord, Author and Syndicated
Beauty Beyond 50 Columnist

☐ *Look Like a Winner After 50 with Care, Color and Style,*
3rd edition. "*Look Like A Winner* is 'must reading' for any woman
wanting to keep the sparkle of youth polished and shining beyond
the fifth decade." $15.95 BOOK

☐ *Feel Nifty After 50! Top Tips to Help Women Grow Young!*
Does your spirit need lifting, your body need lightening, your face
need brightening, your mind need firing? You'll find fuel aplenty
in *Nifty.* $12.95 BOOK

☐ Free catalog

Residents of Colorado sales tax: State 3.8%, Denver County 7.3%

Some of the Low-Cost Special Reports
Featured in Catalog

☐ Beauty Tips for Breast Cancer Survivors. $3 SPECIAL REPORT

☐ How to Get Your Best Overall Look. $3 SPECIAL REPORT

☐ More Than 100 Commonsense Ways to Win the Age Game.
$3 SPECIAL REPORT

☐ *Beauty Beyond 50* columns on Hair Care and Styling.
$3 SPECIAL REPORT

☐ *Beauty Beyond 50* columns on Fashion. $3 SPECIAL REPORT

☐ Seven Reasons to Encourage You to Stay Fit. $2 SPECIAL REPORT

☐ Secrets to Keeping Off the Pounds. $3 SPECIAL REPORT

☐ Keep Age Out of Mind and Image. **FREE** with one purchase

Please send your check or money order to

Golden Aspen Publishing
Post Office Box 37033
Denver, CO 80237-0333

Phone 303/694-6555, Fax 303/694-0737, Email GAPub@aol.com